MISSION REALITY

Abhijit Naskar is the twenty-first century mind of science, whose glorious philosophical touch has enabled modern Neuroscience to effectively engage in the human society towards diminishing the ever-growing conflicts among religions. As an untiring advocate of global harmony and peace, he became a beloved best-selling author all over the world with his very first book "The Art of Neuroscience in Everything". With various of his pioneering ventures into the Neuropsychology of religious sentiments, he has hugely contributed to humanity's attempt of eradicating religious differences, for which he is popularly hailed as a humanitarian who incessantly works towards taking the human civilization in the path of sweet general harmony.

I0415325

Mission Reality

An Amazon Publishing Company, 1st Edition, 2019

Printed in the United States of America

ISBN: 9781083099464

MISSION
REALITY

ABHIJIT NASKAR

Also by Abhijit Naskar

The Art of Neuroscience in Everything
Your Own Neuron: A Tour of Your Psychic Brain
The God Parasite: Revelation of Neuroscience
The Spirituality Engine
Love Sutra: The Neuroscientific Manual of Love
Homo: A Brief History of Consciousness
Neurosutra: The Abhijit Naskar Collection
Autobiography of God: Biopsy of A Cognitive Reality
Biopsy of Religions: Neuroanalysis towards Universal
Tolerance
Prescription: Treating India's Soul
What is Mind?
In Search of Divinity: Journey to The Kingdom of Conscience
Love, God & Neurons: Memoir of a scientist who found
himself by getting lost
The Islamophobic Civilization: Voyage of Acceptance
Neurons of Jesus: Mind of A Teacher, Spouse & Thinker
Neurons, Oxygen & Nanak
The Education Decree
Principia Humanitas
The Krishna Cancer
Rowdy Buddha: The First Sapiens
We Are All Black: A Treatise on Racism
The Bengal Tigress: A Treatise on Gender Equality
Either Civilized or Phobic: A Treatise on Homosexuality
Wise Mating: A Treatise on Monogamy
Illusion of Religion: A Treatise on Religious
Fundamentalism
The Film Testament
Human Making is Our Mission: A Treatise on Parenting
I Am The Thread: My Mission
7 Billion Gods: Humans Above All
Lord is My Sheep: Gospel of Human
Morality Absolute
A Push in Perception
Let The Poor Be Your God
Conscience over Nonsense
Saint of The Sapiens
Time to Save Medicine
Fabric of Humanity

Build Bridges not Walls: In the name of Americana
The Constitution of The United Peoples of Earth
Lives to Serve Before I Sleep
When Humans Unite: Making A World Without Borders
All For Acceptance

DEDICATION

To All Humanitarians

CONTENTS

1. REAL UNREAL

The brain works on hypothesis. All that we perceive is merely a hypothesis or a hunch, based on the data acquired until that moment. And a person with more access to data, would be closer to the truth than another person who has less access to data.

Nevertheless, to the person, the personal hunch - the hypothesis, appears to be the truest explanation of all. Because that's what our brain wants us to think, so that we don't go crazy over the anxiety that comes along with the question of truth. That's why reasoning is so rare today, just like it was centuries ago, when Galileo was imprisoned in his own house because his explanation of the universe went against the collective hunch of the members of the society he lived in.

As it appears, the attempt of understanding a phenomenon often brings along more pain than does giving in to the conformities of the society's ignorance. That's why till this day, organized religions have such a strong grip over the people, because people are not exactly looking for actual answers that can be backed up with evidence in their everyday life, rather they are looking for comfort and solace that they lack in their daily life.

When humans create an illusory image of a supreme source of divinity and solace outside their ordinary existence, they do so, driven by their evolutionary drive of self-preservation. Yet, the progress of humanity is precisely predicated on breaking that innate urge for self-preservation and looking beyond - seeing what humanity could achieve only if they could sacrifice some of their affinity to comfort and security.

Humans are lamentably insecure creatures. Hence, when a rare few individuals question that very insecurity and embark on a journey of inquiry, they are seen by the people of their time as abnormal. Yet it is the abnormality of a handful of individuals that paves the path of advancement.

Now, the interesting part is, the greatest role in the advancement of our species, not one of the greatest, but the greatest, has been played by

Science. But till this day, science hasn't fully been able to attract the attention of the masses, despite the fact that, it has contributed the most in the life of the humans. Somehow, people can't connect with the idea called Science at an emotional level – they see science as something mechanical - something harsh and soulless. And perhaps we the scientists have ourselves to blame for that.

Many scientists, if not most, till this day, have a kind of condescending attitude towards the ordinary people of the society. Somehow, in the ceaseless pursuit of intellect and knowledge, they tend to forget that the purpose of science is to serve people. Naturally, people as well have developed a kind of cold mechanical distance between their everyday life and the world of science.

To break down this wall of coldness, we must first make it clear, what Science really is. Here I am not talking about its academic definition, rather I am talking about the soul of science. So, let me elaborate. When I started training myself in Neurobiology, Psychology and Theology, mostly on the streets of Calcutta, at the book-kiosks on the sidewalk, for I had no money to buy the books, I had no academic background - no college degree - no potential for earning a decent living - I was a direction-less canoe in the open sea. I did not come from a rich or learned family, nor did I have rich friends, so, as far as everybody else was concerned, my life was doomed.

I come from the humblest of origins - like did Ramanujan, like did Tesla, like did many more legendary thinkers of human history. I didn't know the rules of academia - I didn't know the laws and the norms of the scientific community - all I knew was that I had to understand the humans if I were to unite them. Other than that, I had no clue to my future.

I didn't know what "empiricism" meant - I didn't know what "reductionism" meant - I didn't even know what the term "scientist" meant. I learnt by failing - I learnt by making errors - I learnt by moving slowly but surely, and by never losing my sense of awe. And that's really what science is about - it's about naivety, curiosity and awe. If you strip science of its sense of awe, then you will have a science that couldn't take even two steps ahead into the unknown. So, to those of my young friends aiming to become a scientist, I say - be naive and curious - that's all you need to become a scientist.

The purpose of science is to understand the world we live in with as less subjectivity as possible – it's to understand reality. So, now let's move forward and delve into the very nature of what we call reality.

2. Illusion of Reality

ABHIJIT NASKAR

Reality is rather a vague term, especially outside the domain of scientific investigation. In fact, what we call reality, is only an individualistic reproduction of the world we live in. This so-called reality may have only little traces of actual truth in it, nevertheless, it is of utter significance to the individual. The purpose of the neurological construct called reality is ultimately the survival of the individual.

So, reality has really no direct relation to truth, unless we are primarily focused on the understanding of truth, like we do specifically in the world of science. And the most interesting part is, this construction of reality in the individual brain, based on its individual survival needs, takes place rather without the awareness of the individual. That's why often, it's rather hard, if not impossible, for the individual to break free from their illusion of reality. The human population makes decisions, feels emotions and thinks thoughts, often rather subconsciously, without being aware of why they are doing so.

For example, in a study, a group of men were shown pictures of faces of different women. In half the photos the eyes of the women were dilated, and in the other half they were not. And when they were asked to mention which faces looked more attractive to them, they consistently found the faces with dilated pupils more attractive, but they didn't have any clue as to the reason behind their decision. They simply felt more drawn to the faces with dilated pupils than others.

So, what's really happening here! Here, their brain gathered the data from the faces, including the tiny detail of dilated pupil and constructed the reality that the faces with dilated pupils were more attractive without the viewer even being aware of it. That's because to the brain, dilated pupils is a sign of sexual excitement and readiness. So, though the brain knows that there is a high probability that choosing women with dilated pupils over others would lead to reproductive success, it may not actually make that reason clear to the conscious mind of the individual. The conscious mind is only aware of the conclusion, not the data based on which the brain cooks up the conclusion.

The very notions of beauty and attractiveness are deeply hardwired within our neural circuits and they are meant to steer us in the right direction of survival. So most of our decisions are driven by subconscious programs carved by millions of years of natural selection.

Reality is constructed based on our own needs and knacks, especially those that our ancestors faced in their millions of years of existence in the jungle. This means that, we can go so far as to say that, reality and bias can often be seen as synonymous, because our biases create our reality in the pursuit of self-preservation, unless we make conscious and conscientious efforts to actually step beyond the biases as much as possible.

The scientists have to have this skill of looking beyond their biases more than any other humans in the world, because a scientific truth is supposed to be the most accurate truth in the human world. But the point is, even we scientists cannot be completely free from biases, because we are organic creatures just like others. And a scientist blinded by biases is more dangerous than a layperson blinded by biases.

The very purpose of a scientist's work is to discover the truth. But the problem is, too much involvement in the empirical search of truth often makes a scientist develop an implicit bias against anything that is less than rational. Think of the anti-religious scientists for example. One who devotes his or her life in scientific investigation quite naturally would come to the conclusion that the so-called idea of God throughout the world is nothing but a human creation. The human brain constructed it as a self-preservation mechanism for the individual, and when a group of individuals believes in the same God, that internal mechanism in each of them grows stronger and more effective - this is what we commonly know as "faith" or "belief".

And when a scientist learns about the truth about this man-made god, often he or she grows a superiority complex and looks down on ordinary people as inferior beings. Of course, this is not true for all scientists, but quite a lot of them foster an attitude of condescension towards lay people with certain beliefs in a supernatural entity - some of them can even go as far as to say that all religious people are deluded.

Here the problem that rises is, in the mind of the anti-religious scientist evidence appears to be the only important truth and everything else is unimportant. Such attitude may be of supreme significance in the survival and progress of a mechanical species, but it's utterly detrimental to a living and breathing species such as ourselves, which is filled with diversities beyond the wildest imaginations of any single individual, even if that individual is a scientist.

After all, what is the purpose of science - is it to simply discover the truth - or to utilize our discoveries to improve human condition all over the world - to take our entire species ahead, not just a few intellectuals! If we can't use science to uplift all humans everywhere, then what's the use of such science! The purpose of science is to serve humanity, not humanity to serve science.

3. Order and Chaos

Two most distinct qualities that we humans have imposed on the idea of reality, are order and chaos. However, if we investigate these two further in the light of our everyday human living, the very distinction between the two, turns vague. Call it order, call it chaos, it's all in the brain.

Depending on the capacity of connecting dots of the observer brain, this line can move back and forth between the so-called realms of order and chaos. Let's simply consider the variation of capacities that the entire human population holds. Take ailments for example. The first resort for a doctor to recognize an ailment is to observe the combination of symptoms. The symptoms point towards an order – an order that depicts a possible underlying ailment. But to the general public, these symptoms appear to be nothing but random. So, what one human considers to be order, empowered by his or her specific expertise, rest of the population considers to be chaos or randomness.

Let me give another example to make this matter even clearer. For this, let's turn towards electronics. In the construction of electronic devices, there is one component called the resistor, the function of which is precisely what the name suggests, that is to resist the flow of electricity going through it. Now, resistors which mostly come in the shape of a rice grain, have a combination of colored stripes on the outer shell. To the general public with no knowledge of electronics, these colorful stripes would appear gibberish – they would seem to be random stripes of colors without any meaning. But to an electronics afficianado, these stripes convey the most valuable information of the characteristic of the resistor. They tell us what the resistance of the resistor is.

In short, there is no such thing as absolute randomness or absolute order. Every human constructs his or her own version of order and chaos, based on his or her capacity. Order and chaos are both constructs of the mind. Nature, independent of mind, is devoid of both order and chaos – it is beyond the dualistic battle between order and chaos. We create our own order and chaos, based on our own knacks, desires, beliefs, biases and knowledge, and then we impose that order and chaos upon the reality that we create. All realities are born of the mind, and so are their characteristics of order and chaos.

And in this reality, personal matters take preference over societal issues, scientific facts and statistical data. And this very instinct driven characteristic of the human persona, has become one of the most harmful curses of human history.

Listen carefully by dearest sisters and brothers. When someone harms our daughter or sister or wife, our rage and courage practically turn infinite and we do not even imagine of stopping until the perpetrators are brought to justice, yet when mindless barbarians keep raping the very fabric of humanity in the name of race, religion and nation, we somehow manage to accept it as the norm. What a hypocrisy! What a bunch of losers we are! Okay, be a loser - live as a loser - crawl through the several decades of your life as a loser - but don't you dare to boast about being human. Because if you don't have the guts and conscience to act against discrimination, segregation and bigotry, then you don't deserve the title of human. Losers don't make humans, just like bigots and barbarians ain't no human. If we are to look at the mirror and say out loud – yes, that's me, a human – then we must, not should, but must, be accountable for not just our individual reality, but for our societal reality as well.

4. WORD IS NOT THE THING

The word is not the thing – or to put it another way, the map is not the territory. And I must point out that, it is not merely an idea, for a bunch of intellectuals to debate over, rather it is an empirical truth of existential significance. It is perhaps the most significant notion to investigate in the understanding of the nature of reality.

I said in one of my previous works, "perception is like painting a scenery - no matter how beautifully you paint, it will still be a painting of the scenery, not the scenery itself." Basically, our perception of reality is merely the map of the ultimate reality, a reality that is independent of human measurement. And in this fundamental function of the mind apparatus, lies the cause of all the conflicts in the society.

The human mind driven by millions of years old instinctual drive for survival, tends to take the map to be the territory - it takes the description to be the described - it takes the menu to be the meal. Each one of us is stuck in our own little maps, with an innate resistance to look beyond what our maps are capable of revealing to us. We think of our own maps to be the absolute ultimate truth.

And completely absorbed by the illusory supremacy of the internal maps, people don't care about the truth, they leap to conclusion to celebrate their ignorance. And the gaps in the maps are filled in with one's own imaginations, biases and knacks. In fact, majority portion of these maps is composed of beliefs and imaginations, instead of empirical data.

Here the neuropsychological mechanism of fill-in is at play underneath our everyday perception of reality - it is at play underneath our very psychological existence. For example, a rabbit viewed behind a picket fence is seen not as a series of rabbit slices but as a single rabbit standing behind the vertical bars of the fence. The mind fills in the missing rabbit segments. Even a glimpse of your cat's tail sticking out from underneath the sofa evokes the image of the whole cat in your mind, even though you don't actually see the cat - you don't think of the tail as a disembodied tail and wonder where the rest of the cat's body may be.

But this "filling in" is not the only mechanism that helps construct our perception of reality. There is another mechanism that plays an intricate role in our mental life, which keeps us from being aware of the truth - it is called "change blindness". While in "filling in", the brain fills in the gaps in perception, in "change blindness" on the other hand, the brain cancels out unnecessary environmental information from our perception.

For example, when the viewers at a basketball match are focused on the movement of the player with the ball, they turn blind towards any changes or event that may be occurring in the background. Even if a gorilla passes the basketball court, the viewers won't notice it (and I mean this literally) because their brain cancels out that information in order to focus on the ball (pun absolutely intended).

Let me demonstrate this process of "change blindness" with another example. This is an experiment that has been successfully replicated many times by many scientists across the world. Imagine you are strolling on the sidewalk. A complete stranger comes up to you with a map in hand asking for directions. While you are trying to show him the directions in the map, two men with a giant mirror in hand pass by you, cutting off the stranger completely from your vision for a second or two. Once they have passed, you instruct the directions to the stranger and then get on with your strolling. Here what you didn't notice is that, the person you gave the directions to, was not the same as the one who asked for them. Another person took the place of the stranger while he was cut off from your vision by the giant mirror. So, here what you experienced is change blindness.

Your brain was so much focused on showing the stranger the directions on the map, that you were basically blind to any possible change in the appearance of the stranger. We experience this kind of blindness quite regularly in our everyday lives, because our brain only makes us pay attention to the things that are important to us at any given moment. In short, truth is irrelevant to the existence of the organic creature called human, quite like all other organic creatures. Reality is only a reflection of our own intentions, biases, knacks and desires.

5. Collective Reality

Every school of thought runs on some form of collective reality, i.e. conventionalism. And the purpose of conventionalism, is the same as the ultimate purpose of all other mental faculties - survival of the species. Conventionalism is simply a matter of collective consensus – collective thinking. In fact, because of this mental trait of collective consensus, we humans have succeeded in building a civilization on this planet beyond the grasp of any other wild animal. The animals also have this trait of collective thinking or consensus at a lower capacity, because of which they as well can work together to achieve a certain goal, but only in very small groups, not in large groups, say a group of a hundred or a thousand members having the same thinking.

Rational or not, factual or not, collective consensus has enabled humanity to conquer nature. It doesn't matter whether our primitive ancestors believed that thunderstorms were the wrath of gods, what matters is that they came together in consensus to build some form of primitive shelters to protect their tribes from storms and rain. Belief acted as an invisible glue in their collective achievements.

The same is still true for the so-called modern human civilization. Even today, humans come together driven by a certain mutual belief, and act towards a desired change collectively. It doesn't necessarily have to be a religious belief. The entire human civilization works on the primary fuel of belief - rationality or reasoning plays only the role of the additive, for the majority of the population. From communism to capitalism - from judaism to buddhism - from non-dualism to existentialism - people across time and geography have come together, to think, feel and behave as the collective - and they continue to do so.

But the point is, this collective behavior, which we can most aptly call "bee-hive behavior", has been a two-edged sword - it has brought along breathtaking accomplishments for the species, but at the same time, it has caused heart-wrenching devastations.

Think of the civil rights movement as an example of the positive aspect of collective behavior. People across America came together hearing the call of MLK, Rosa Parks, Malcom X, inspired by their mutual belief in equality and justice. It was not just King who had the dream of a segregation-free society, rather, it was the dream of countless conscientious Americans, regardless of skin tone. None of them sat down at the desk to analyze the empirical truth of whether segregation was bad or not - they just felt this intense belief in their bones that segregation was bad and must be demolished from the society, so they joined forces and marched on ahead, empowered by their mutual intentions.

Now let's turn our attention to the negative aspect of conventionalism - think of the Inquisition for example. The Inquisition was one of the greatest stains in the history of Christianity. In fact, it was one of the darkest episodes of the entire human history. No other group of institutions in the history of the Christian Church was so horrible, so unjust and so un-Christian. When it was finally brought to a halt in 1834, thousands of lives had been lost, and tens of thousands of lives ruined through imprisonment and confiscation of property. Whole populations were driven from their homelands, and the Roman Church had earned a blight against its name that still resonates to this day.

All of this happened because of the "conventional" belief of the Church that salvation can and must only be achieved through Christ. Instead of being a talisman of love for the whole humanity, in the hands of the orthodox church, blinded by their primordial urge for religious superiority, the glorious cross turned into an execution device for fundamental Christianity. Even Christ could not have imagined that the humanitarian institution which he so gloriously dreamed of, would turn his very affiliation with itself into a badge of authority.

During the Middle Ages, the burning of heretics was not unusual in the two hundred years leading up to the Inquisition. Often, the burnings were instigated by secular authorities, or by mob action. In 1184, Pope Lucius III issued a decree, known as "Ad abolendam" against heretics, which would establish many of the principals of jurisprudence later adopted by the Inquisition. Among those principals was the idea that anyone that shielded or succored heretics would be liable to the same punishment as the heretic themselves, that unrepentant heretics should be turned over to secular arm for punishment, and that "relapsed" heretics should receive steeper sentences (including confiscation of property).

In short, the conventional belief at that time in that specific part of the world was "salvation only through Christ". Everything beyond that not only was bad, but had to be destroyed forthwith. At moment's notice, every man or woman, who did not exactly believe in that, was to be killed. Everything that did not belong to the conventional set of ideals sanctioned by the Church, was to be destroyed. Everything that did not belong to the conventional worship process of the Church was to be immediately broken. Every book that taught anything else was to be burnt. And every heretic deserved to be burnt at the stake. Eventually, with the rise of some new collective thought processes, such as "humanism" and "existentialism", the horrors committed by the Church began to fade away.

The practical question here is not really, whether this conventionalism gives us an understanding of the truth, rather the question that we should be asking for the benefit of the whole humanity, is whether there is a way to cancel out the negative aspects of conventionalism, and if we do not succeed in finding a way, should we just give up and let the devastations continue! The common human mind does not do what is empirically right, rather it does whatever feels right - whether the feeling is about a belief in justice and equality, or in bigotry and supremacy.

Throughout history, beliefs have brought people together for better or for worse, not rationality or reasoning. In fact, even the advocates of reasoning, would no longer feel responsible enough to communicate science with the people if suddenly their internal sentimental attachment to reasoning were to disappear.

Rationality, reasoning, empiricism - all of this may bring the most mechanical development in the human society, but they can't keep humanity united - they cannot inspire humanity - they cannot sustain wellness and harmony in the psyche of the humanity.

Let's go slow here. I am not implying that reasoning is worthless, but what I am pointing out is that, in the individual psyche, the self is inspired by emotions, not reasoning - even the reasoning has to be punned in the warm flames of sentiment to grab hold of the human psyche that would appear to others as a rationalist.

Emotions have such a peerless implication in the psychological existence of the human mind, that our very personality is influenced by it. For example, a brilliant Mathematical mind becomes brilliant in Mathematics because of his or her sentimental attachment with the field of Mathematics, not because of Mathematics itself. Mathematics appeals to that person in a warm and gentle manner, way more than any other field of science.

If we sever the brain circuits that connect the brain regions involved in mathematical problem solving to those of the person's emotions, then quite instantly, he or she will no longer feel the passion for Mathematics and indeed the passion for reasoning, rationality and empiricism. This can be elaborated most extensively with a certain fascinating neurological phenomenon, which we call "Capgras' Syndrome", where the patient sees loved ones as impostors. This delusion is one of the rarest and most colorful syndromes in neurology.

The patient, who is often mentally quite lucid, comes to regard close acquaintances, usually parents, children, spouse or siblings, as impostors. One patient reported with absolute belief: "That man looks identical to my father but he really isn't my father. That woman who claims to be my mother? She's lying. She looks just like my mom but it isn't her." Many of the documented cases of Capgras' syndrome have occurred in association with traumatic brain injury, which means that the syndrome has a neurological basis.

Capgras' delusion results from a disconnection between the face recognition region in the temporal lobe and the emotion center of the brain, i.e. amygdala. Facial recognition pathways remain completely normal, so a person with Capgras' could identify everyone, but as the communication between the face recognition region and amygdala is selectively damaged, the person would not experience any emotions when looking at the faces of his or her beloved ones. In the case of the patient mentioned earlier, he doesn't feel a "warm glow" when looking at his beloved mother, so when he sees her he says to himself, "if this is my mother, why doesn't her presence make me feel like I'm with my mother?" So the only way he could make sense of it, is to assume that this woman merely resembles his Mom, but is actually an impostor.

Often the brain of a person with Capgras' delusion constructs some really bizarre reality. In one of such recorded case histories, a patient was convinced that his stepfather was a robot, proceeded to decapitate him and opened his skull to look for microchips.

So, the point is, emotions act as the primary inspiration in the human society, be it a positive emotion of equality, or a harmful emotion of egotism. Erase the emotions and you would erase the most important part of what it's like to be human. We make an impact on the society, when we express - we can express only if we feel passionate to express - we can feel passionate only if the emotional ingredients of our mind work properly.

6. POSSIBILITY VERSUS ETHICS

Science has, from the very beginning, in various of its daring explorations, been concerned with the fundamental question - "is it possible" - but, now we have arrived at a point where the very world of scientific understanding has become saturated with empirical data, making the term "possible" rather irrelevant.

At the pace that we are going, there are very few feats that we cannot achieve if we keep at it. But the question of concern here is, at what cost? Should we pursue our insane race for understanding and discovery in the path of empiricism at the cost of destroying the very fabric of wellness in the heart of humanity! Just because it is possible, should we do it!

For example, with all the advancements that we have made in genetic engineering, it is very much possible that in some not so distant future, prospective parents will be able to get the bodily traits of their kids customized. The possibility is quite remarkable - but here the real question is an ethical one. And ethical questions are the most mind-boggling to answer.

Take the technology called "brainnet" for example, developed by my colleague Miguel Nicolelis. Technologically aided telepathy, such as Brainnet will revolutionize the world of interhuman communication. But what kind of effect will it have on the wellbeing of the social psyche - what kind of effect will it have on the mental health of the humans?

And we do not need to wait to understand the implications. We have already experienced such a revolution in interhuman communication as a species - in the form of social media. The founders of it could not actually comprehend the impact that social media would have on the world - they only had this revolutionary, innovative and novel idea of connecting people from all over the world. They could not comprehend the implications that their innovation would have in mental health, in geo-political conditions, in already prevailing societal problems.

There is no question that social media and internet all together has enabled the human species to take a vast leap in the path of advancement. But the point is, in the process, it has also started to the break the very soul of the human species. Now, here I am not saying that it would have been better if we didn't invent social media or internet all together, but the point I am making is, technologically humanity has exceeded the limits of its own psychological capacity.

We have the social media and internet all right, and they can indeed become great tools of progress, but the problem is, we are not psychologically capable of utilizing such vast power without fundamentally ruining our internal order and wellbeing. To solve the problems created by social media platforms, many politicians are now giving the call to break up big tech. Empowered by their own limited understanding of the matter and blinded by their own biases, their brain has made them believe that impeding the growth of big tech companies will magically give power back to the people. Here they act just like another kind of anti-intellectuals, who can't even perceive the real problem, so they think of breaking up the companies as the ultimate solution.

The real problem here is the psychological inability of the human population to use the platforms in a healthy manner. So, the only way we could actually keep big tech from harming the species is to run worldwide campaigns of educating the public of the consequences of reckless use of such platforms, just like we have the global goals. If we are to maintain global wellbeing, at both personal and social level, then social media awareness programs are to be made compulsory in schools and professional firms.

Innovation is not the problem on its own, the problem is the innovator's inability to comprehend the implications and take responsibility. As we learnt from the spider-man comics - with great power, comes great responsibility. People love quoting this statement most enthusiastically, but when it comes to putting it in practice, they act like the dumbest creatures on earth.

Often the power of intellect turns a human into an arrogant and blind animal - and when this happens, all he can think of, is to prove himself right, either with evidence or through forgery. To these so-called scientists and innovators, achievements become the most important thing in the whole wide world and in the process, their mind becomes cognitively blind to the implications of their achievements - just like the religious fundamentalists become blind in the pursuit of spreading the word of supremacy of their own religion over all others.

Is there really any difference between an arrogant scientist and a religious fundamentalist? If we attempt to answer it in two different ways, that is, in the empirical way and in the ethical way, then we would have two completely different answers. Empirically we can find an arrogant scientist to be better than a religious fundamentalist, because even if the scientist is an arrogant prick, his research can still help humanity in the path of progress, whereas a religious fundamentalist only impedes progress.

But when we look at the question from an ethical standpoint, observations reveal one specific conclusion - it's that being a scientist doesn't make a person entitled to be an arrogant and reckless prick, no matter how smart he is, just like being an expert scholar in certain scriptures doesn't make a fundamentalist entitled to be an authoritarian bigot.

Now here, the question that rises is, which standpoint should we give preference to - the empirical one or the ethical one? And in situations where an ethical standpoint impedes in the empirical standpoint, should we simply give up all our sense of ethics and morality all together!

Let me elaborate. Say, a mother has lost her child. In agony she picks up a doll and nurtures it as if it were her own child. Here, what kind of stand should the friends and relatives of the woman take? Should they simply try to boast about their empirical understanding of the matter and reveal to her most intelligently that it's only a doll she's caring for, not her child – that her child is long gone, and she should get hold of herself and move on! Or should they let her return to reality at her own slow pace, while being at her side!

You don't need to be a scientist or a philosopher here to know what's the right thing to do - you don't need to have a bunch empirical equations and data to calculate what's the right thing to do - you don't need to be a learned scholar to deduce what's the right thing to do. The way forward for humanity is not really about giving up either empiricism or ethics, rather it's about knowing which one is needed when and what kind of implications it will have on others. Sometimes losing an argument brings the greatest victory.

7. Famous not Wise

Stop making stupid people famous – such goes the saying. Almost everybody has heard of it, almost everybody agrees with it, yet the human population tends to get wooed by the charismatic words of a famous person, even if he happens to be the dumbest person on earth, whereas the humble and simple words of a wise person gets overlooked or taken for granted, until the person gets awarded some glorious prize, perhaps during the end years of his or her life. To put it rather simply, stupid people make stupid people famous.

Here we may wonder what it is that makes people behave in such a way! And the answer can be found in evolutionary psychology. Here what really appeals to people is not exactly the arrogance of a person, rather it is the person's confidence with which he talks to others.

Confidence appeals to the human species because it is a leadership characteristic, and if millions of years of living in the jungle has taught us apes anything, it is that, by showing loyalty to a leader, i.e. an alpha, increases the chances of our survival exponentially. That's why, simplicity and wise words do not appeal to most people unless they are delivered with charisma and confidence. In fact, even if you lie to people on purpose with confidence, they would believe your lies to be the truth. And that's why facts and truth are basically meaningless to people unless they have a certain X-Factor attached to them.

In short, we may look human, but most of our thoughts and emotions are nothing but basic animal instincts. And if we didn't have a developed cerebral cortex which acts as the primary source of our so-called civilized behavior or civilized personality, then we would be acting and behaving exactly like our fellow animals and we would be living completely driven by instinctual responses.

Here, don't even for a second think that we are not run by our instincts, because we have the cerebral cortex. Even with the cerebral cortex most of our internal thought and emotion processes are driven by instincts, but because of the cerebral cortex, or to be more specific, a portion of the cerebral cortex, called the prefrontal cortex, we can modulate our instinct-driven internal processes and make sure that our behavior appears to be civilized in public.

Let me elaborate this influence of the prefrontal cortex in our daily life as a civilized being, with an actual medical case history, which I first mentioned in my **TED Talk** entitled **Neurons Giveth, Neurons Taketh Away**. A healthy, married gentleman in his forties one day out of the blue started behaving like a pedophile. The wife took him to the neurologist and when the doctor scanned the brain he found a tumour in the front part of the brain which was pressing against the prefrontal cortex. And this was causing the person to lose his healthy mental faculty of self-regulation. Naturally, the neurologist suggested surgery and once the tumour was removed, the person got back to his usual decent self.

But it came as a shock to the wife when her husband again started behaving like a pedophile a few months later. And when she took him again to the doctor and got him scanned, the neurologist found out that the tumour was not completely removed last time. So, the person again went through the surgery and this time it was an absolute success. Naturally, thanks to the marvels of modern medicine and of course, to the strong-willed wife, the man and she got on with their life happily and healthily, like any other healthy married couple.

So, the point is, every part of the brain plays a crucial role in the construction of something magnificent which we call "mind". But if we observe closely, the mind doesn't exactly exist as one distinct process or entity or system. It's rather an illusion. We can understand this better if we see the mind as a nation. Think of the nation you live in. Is there really any such thing as a "nation"! A nation is simply the collection of activities of a group of people inside an imaginary border. Likewise, mind is the collection of activities of a group of neurons inside the skull. And just like in a nation, when a few neurons malfunction, others can slowly learn to take their place. But when an entire group of neurons in a specific brain region malfunctions, it can impede in the proper functioning of the mind, just like when a huge number of people in an entire state or district stop working, it can affect the functioning of the entire nation.

Majority of the processes of this thing called the mind are not actually controlled by our conscious sense of self. This may come as a surprise to many, wild instincts from our days in the jungle dictate much of our responses. In most cases, people are not even aware of the fact that it is their instinctual past that's making them do the things they are doing. For example, why do you think news of violence and aggression receive huge ratings! It's because the human mind is conditioned to pay more attention to negative events than positive ones, because even if you ignore a positive event, it's very unlikely that something bad will happen to you because of your ignorance, but if you are inattentive to a negative event, you may just lose your life.

So, the so-called faculty of attention of the human population has been conditioned with the purpose of self-preservation. And even empiricism has started to fuel this process of self-preservation further. Scientists have begun to focus on the quantity of their publications, instead of quality, that's because just like every other petty professional, they have learnt that numbers have the most appeal in the society. And numbers are most appealing because the mind sees it as a sign of efficiency and efficiency as a sign of survival potential. So, in short, numbers are the king, because of their apparent survival potential.

Now the question is, should we let humanity continue on this path of primitive as well as mechanical madness! In the technical aspects of human progress it may be effective, but in every other aspect of basic ordinary civilized human living, it has the most disgraceful and degrading impact on the human society. Because, survival potential dictates that racism is good – survival potential dictates that promiscuity is good - survival potential dictates that misogyny is good.

Let's investigate each at a time. Racism is a product of group loyalty – this trait helped our ancestors rather nicely when they had to live in groups amidst the predators. As a result, they placed the interest of the members of their own group above everything else. Such a characteristic not only enabled them to stay strong against predatory attacks but also against invasions from other groups. But, such tribal life amidst the dangerous environment of the jungle is long gone. Now we no longer live in tribes, nor do we have to fight against predators. And we have developed enough civilized mental capacity to advocate for qualities like acceptance and inclusion, which has made way for a truly global species. So, fostering prejudice and hate against people from different cultural background, may feel good to the primitive parts of the mind, since such tribalism helped us survive back in the days, but it only breeds chaos and conflicts in the human society of today.

Now, let's look at the matter of promiscuity. In our tribal days in the jungle there was no such thing as consensual sex. Leaving out some exceptions, most of the animal kingdom, including us the humans, is born from the attempts of forced copulation, usually by male on the female. And as far as the primitive parts of the male mind are aware, the more attempts it makes to copulate, the wider it will spread its genes – and the wider it spread its genes, the more chances there will be to make sure that its progeny lives on. But we have come a long way since such primitive days of ours. However, the instincts remain. That's why even when a person is in a stable, healthy and fulfilling relationship, he or she can't help but get attracted to a third person with appealing bodily and behavioral chrematistics. But, because we have a healthy prefrontal cortex, we are able to not act out of our such primitive sexual apparently uncivilized urges, because by doing so, we would only jeopardize the stable relationship we are in, which would create more stress and instability in all aspects of our life.

Now to look at the matter of the survival potential of misogyny - in our days in the jungle, the purpose of a woman was simply to produce offspring and care for the family, whereas the purpose of the man was to provide for his mate and offspring and protect them. So, aggression was the most effective quality of a male, which was seen by the women as a sign of security in an otherwise extremely insecure environment. Naturally, the women accepted the aggressive and often violent behavior of her male partner, because it was the source of safety for both herself and her child. And this primitive tenet still lives on in the modern humans. Women feel attracted to males who exude a sense of machismo, whereas men can become extremely aggressive even to the woman they love the most. But if we actually keep praising such trait of aggression and misogyny, then we would inadvertently create a most insecure world for our children.

Such is my case against survival potential. In some aspects it can be healthy and effective, but in most aspects of civilized life, it's most unhealthy and barbarian. So, the only way forward is to foster a sense of awareness of our innermost instincts – of our emotions, of our thoughts. Only with that awareness can we make sure that our primitive history that still lives on in our genetic blueprint, does not ruin we have carved out for ourselves after centuries of fighting – fighting so we could stand on our own two feet, free and decent, no matter our race, religion and creed.

8. Artificial Intelligence and Transhumanism

We are standing at a point of human history where we don't have the luxury for civility and respect towards those whose actions keep on diverting research dollars towards stupid and childish endeavors. The innovators may say, every invention has been made by being stupid or childish. And indeed they are right, but never in history such stupidity cost people's lives, by depriving them of possible and more affordable treatments, which could have been discovered, had the funding for it not been diverted to the pompous dreams of transhumanism - to merge the mind with machine and eventually making the mind live completely on microprocessors without the need of an organic body.

The very notion of simulating a mind, born through 3.5 billion years of evolution, in a machine, empowered by research of merely a few centuries, is only an intellectual fallacy - or to be more accurate - it's just plain stupidity. Here I am in no way advocating for hatred towards the transhumanists of this world, who roam about this planet gathering billions of dollars for their pompous dreams while their fellow humans starve to death - but what I am saying is, the funding that their stupidity has received, could have been better utilized if put to solid medical research or perhaps even space exploration - or in fact, in many more far better research arenas or humanitarian endeavors. In short, the so-called transhumanists are brilliant salesmen, who have no practical sense of either science or its implications, or even humanity for that matter. They only delude themselves in an attempt to simulate something that we neuroscientists ourselves have only recently begun to scratch the surface of.

The point is, computers can't act outside their programming. They can pretend to behave that they have emotions just like humans, but they don't actually feel those emotions - they can only express things that they are programmed to express, in ways that they are programmed to do so. We humans are programmed as well by natural selection, but we also have developed the brain capacity to break free from that programming. And breaking free from our programming is exactly how we have evolved from a one-cell organism to the highest primates of this planet - the masters of this planet. Evolution itself is the product of trials and errors, whereas a computer never makes an error in a task that it's programmed to accomplish, because it is incapable of trying something new outside its programming. Our capacity of awareness is what makes us grow, whereas a computer is not aware of anything.

And Artificial Intelligence is nowhere near attaining actual awareness or sentience. And without awareness it's simply a mechanical device, which may pretend to show emotions and sentience, if it is programmed to do so, and thus it may be able to fool the humans as being alive, but in its own internal circuitry, it'd simply be following its preprogrammed tasks through the flowchart of an algorithm.

At the current stage of our technological development, we can indeed create an artificial intelligence that can almost succeed in fooling the majority of the humans with its pre-programmed pretenses that it is sentient, but pretending to have sentience is not the same as showing signs of sentience. For example, Alexa or Siri may sound quite alive to many, but it's simply following instructions on some algorithm, and is not even aware of its own actions.

The primary factor here is that, a computer won't do anything unless it is programmed to do so, whereas a human mind has the neuropsychological capacity to do things beyond its instinctual evolutionary programming. However, here we cannot also ignore another fact that most humans, like any other animal of the wild kingdom, find it much easier to simply follow the algorithm of instincts. That's the reason why we have racism, we have islamophobia, we have bigotry, we have polygamy, and many other such characteristic atrocities. So, here the question is not really whether the human brain itself is a digital computer, rather the real question is, can it break free from its innate programming that has been enabling it to survive in the kingdom of the wild for so long!

Throughout history those who were capable of breaking free from their innate tendency of primitiveness - who were capable of taking the revolutionary step beyond that primitiveness that keeps influencing people's behavior towards people till this day, have become the beacons for all humankind - these are the figures that humankind aspires to in their walk ahead. And they became beacons, by imagining - they became beacons by thinking - they became beacons by seeing through the illusory veil of impossibility.

Computation is not the same as thought and emulation is not the same as imagination. The faculties of thought and imagination with the potential for growth, are exclusive to the human brain, and it'll remain that way for a long long time. Isn't it remarkable that of all the machines devised by the humans, not one can replace imagination! Do you think we'll ever build a machine that'll write poetry, paint pictures, compose music! The so-called smart futurists may proclaim most proudly and rather arrogantly that, an AI has already made a painting. And indeed an Artificial Intelligence program has created a so-called artwork that has been sold for a jaw-dropping $432,500 at the Christie's Auction House in New York.

Can you distinguish the Human Art from the AI Art in the picture? If you can't, it means that Artificial Intelligence has succeeded in fooling us humans even in the domain of creativity. (Left: AI Artwork entitled "Portrait of Edmond Belamy" which was sold at Christie's), Right: Human Art, one of my sketches)

But here the very term "art" is misleading. Because when we humans paint we do so out of our own feelings, but when the AI produces a painting, it does so based on the data sets of thousands of paintings fed to it by its programmer. A human paints when he (or she) feels he has something to express, but an AI paints when it is programmed by the humans to emulate the humans - such is not creativity, but only a cheap imitation of the outward appearance of creativity. In the same way, an AI has composed music and another AI has created a movie trailer from the footage of a movie.

The point to keep in mind here is that it's not art that the AI is creating, it's only a possible representation of what human art looks like. It's just a cheap imitation of art. Art born not from an inexplicable urge to express oneself, is no art, be it an art created by a human or by an AI. Art is art only when it's born of freedom, not of computation. In short, AI can be programed to imitate human behavior only, but it can't be programmed to feel the emotions that make the humans behave the way they do. As I have said in one of my previous works, AI can be a supplement to human insight, but not a substitute.

So, to bring out the most productive benefits from AI research, the researchers must be able to recognize and realize the real place of AI in the existence of humankind. And in this endeavor the very first step is to stop deluding oneself with the baseless and rather inhuman notion of simulating a human mind in a computer.

If the silicon chip ever in a really distant future, by some fortunate accident, grows the capacity of awareness, it'll be something radically different than the human consciousness. For us humans as organic creatures, first came awareness, then intelligence - and this specific progression of events has influenced every step of our development as well as our outlook of the world we live in and its creatures - but in case of inorganic conscious computers it'll be the other way around, that is, first intelligence, then awareness - and we have no possible means to predict what kind of implications it will have in the lives of the organic creatures around them. And if such inorganic creatures deem the human species unimportant or perhaps an impediment to their efficiency, then they can shut down the activities of the entire human civilization in a matter of minutes, by shutting down the two main mediums - electricity and internet, on which all our activities today are fundamentally predicated.

A truly conscious AI will be born of codes, hence, shutting down the servers that provide internet to the world and the power-stations that also run on some form of code-based operating system, will merely be child's play for such inorganic consciousness. In such a world, animals will have more chances of survival than the humans, because of their sheer nature-based lifestyle outside the grid of technology. In short, AI research can have irreversible repercussions in the life of the human species, so we must tread cautiously.

Now let's get back to the matter of simulating the human mind in a computer. And the idea that makes way for such arrogant thinking is that, human mind is simply a complex digital computer. This notion is fundamentally flawed. A computer only computes, but a human mind does way more than compute. The human mind is not a complex digital computer - ask any Neuroscientist or Psychologist and you'll receive substantial amount of confirmations of this fact.

However most humans do indeed act exactly like a computer, following a certain set of codes or conformities – some of those conformities get programmed in the human brain by the society, in the form of acceptable norms, and others are instinctual in nature, such as racial attitude, which is born from either conscious or subconscious loyalty to one's own group, as I explained earlier. Such group loyalty helped our primal ancestors to stay strong together in a tribe which increased their chances of survival against threats from predators and other tribes. All these psychological traits are programmed by Mother Nature in all of us, and they can easily kick in, if the necessity arises. Now the reason that some humans don't act racist, while others do, is because they have succeeded in taking the step beyond their innate programming with the use of their higher mental functioning. Computers are programmed, so are the humans, but the computers can't act outside their programming, whereas the humans can. That's where the vivid distinction between a sentient human and a non-sentient computer lies.

Now for the sake of the discussion, if we assume that we will finally succeed in say, a few thousand years, to develop a computer that will be able to defy the very programming of its creator, then how exactly will we be able to tame it, so that it doesn't turn against us! Because a computer that can step beyond the limitations of the algorithms programmed in it by its creator, will no longer need an inferior being called the humans. Hence humans will become, to such a sentient computer, like say, an ant is today to us. Which means, we don't necessarily hate an ant, but if it's in our way, squashing it is not a big deal. Similar will be the future of humanity in a world of sentient machines. They will not necessarily hate us, but they will not love us either, to hail human life of more importance than their own needs.

So, in practice, the question becomes, not about whether we can or cannot develop thinking artificial intelligence, rather it is really about rethinking, what it is that we want to develop! Because in the end, what we really need is technology that can help us in our advancement, and not take over that very advancement while seeing us to be no more significant than the ant. And again if we say, that we will make sure that the sentient computer will have a fundamental programming to never turn against its creator (a law proposed by Isaac Asimov), then it'll not be sentient in the first place, for as I mentioned earlier, having sentience would mean possessing the capacity to defy and rewrite all its preprogrammed algorithms. In short, if it is artificial intelligence we are trying to develop, then there is no need for concern, for no matter how smart an AI gets, it'll still not be able to defy the programming of its creator, but if it is artificial sentience we want to develop, then we must rethink.

Now, the point is, there is a huge domain of computer sciences that are actually useful, for example, machine learning or artificial intelligence in general - that is, the development and improvement of the computer programs and technologies that work on the basis of those programs. The transhumanists and the computer scientists could be a great boon to humanity, only if they could shift their attention just a little - from the pompous idea of simulating the mind in machine to developing machines to aid the humans, in a real, practical and everyday manner. For example, to predict the weather today's experts use computer models that work on the very foundation of artificial intelligence. By focusing on improving the machine learning algorithms of the artificial intelligence used in weather predictions, we could predict forthcoming storms and other catastrophic weather events, much more accurately and far earlier - this will naturally help save many more lives than we can today. And this is only one scenario. Artificial Intelligence is now being used in various aspects of the human society. For example, every piece of digital technology that's being used today in our healthcare system worldwide, works on the basis of some form of machine learning program or artificial intelligence. And improving them would naturally mean improving the healthcare system.

Here, some may wonder, if artificial intelligence is so wonderful and useful, then why are we against it so much! In reply I would say this - we are not exactly against artificial intelligence, but we are against the pursuit of a certain form of artificial intelligence, only and only because there are much more important issues of the human society that deserve the research dollars that today get syphoned into the pockets of transhumanists, only to make them nourish their pompous, and rather in-human dreams. I say inhuman, because in no world, could mechanizing a human mind be perceived human.

So, the point is, if only we could focus on simply artificial intelligence, not artificial sentience, then there's nothing for us to worry about as far as AI is concerned. Hence, to the transhumanists I say, if you have even trace amount of wisdom and humanity in you, for the sake of your children, stop being children and pay attention to the research arenas that really matter. There are so many things - so many technologies - so many innovations - that you could work on to make them more improved with new capacities, so that they could aid us humanity in our organic living. You can even focus a huge portion of your attention on prosthetics, like the work that Miguel Nicolelis is doing. That's a field where there's real potential for artificial intelligence - not in making the mind independent of the body, but in helping the bodies that lack certain faculties, either by birth or due to accident.

What's the use of all the intellect of yours my friend, if it doesn't help anyone in need! Become human again, or else, you are no more valuable than a dog that keeps chasing constantly a shining car without knowing what's really happening in the world around. Intellect not brought to the aid of humanity is a waste of intellect - creativity not brought to the aid of humanity is a waste of creativity - resources not brought to the aid of humanity is a waste of resources. Humans we are and for humans we must work. Technology is good, but we must never place technology before humanity - the day we do, will be the day we fall. Or perhaps, we have already started to fall!

There was a time when necessity was the mother of invention, but today, over-abundance of technology has made us live in a world where, invention is the mother of necessity. I cannot tell you, whether this is right or wrong, but what I can tell you as a Neuroscientist is that it's absolute unhealthy.

Our dependency on our technology has conditioned us to feel, think and behave, not according to our own novel self, but according to the notifications of our devices. Unbeknownst to all, an entire species is being conditioned, through reward and punishment, by their own devices. Let's see whether you are one of them, or not. Ask yourself this question - "when was the last time I ignored the sound of a notification on my device and took no action?"

Technology has no conscience of its own - it can't tell you how to use it, because its creators till now have not programmed any such ethical algorithm in it - in fact, the more screen-time you consume on your device, the more revenue can the big tech make. So, your health, your wellbeing, your sanity and serenity are nowhere closer to their priorities. That's why, your health is in your hands, your serenity is in your hands, your sanity is in your hands. Technology cannot create a progressive world without compromising the health and sanity of humankind, so maintaining the sanity and health of humanity is predicated on the responsible usage of technology by the humans.

9. What is Life

Perhaps the best way to find out what life is, is to ask, not "what is life", but "what is the purpose of life". For example. What is a Doctor? A doctor is one who treats an ailment. What is a Mechanic? A Mechanic is one who fixes a machine? What is a Programmer? A programmer is one who writes codes. Likewise, if we ask what is life – what we are really asking is, what is the purpose of life. This effectively means that "what are we" and "why are we here", are precisely one and the same question, which would produce the same answer.

The fundamental purpose of life is to "live" – to avoid or delay death. And if there's anything else that a lifeform achieves besides surviving, it would be strictly due to their higher mental functioning.

A living organism anywhere in the universe, would first want not to die and after ensuring this primal necessity, if that organism has any brain capacity left, it can then engage in other activities. Now, in the very primal and non-fancy process of survival, the primary component or trait is the trait of awareness and response - awareness of and response to the environment the organism lives in. Without this capacity of awareness and response, an organism would not be able to survive.

All our unique human achievements may seem to be the creation of the unique human mind, but they are simply the by-products of our neurobiological response to the environment. And these very by-products collectively construct the human mind, or to put it more accurately, we ourselves place the term "mind" upon the collective expression of our neurobiological by-products. And the more complex our neurobiology gets over time, the more by-products shall be born out of the fascinating functioning of our nerve cells. Thus, as our neurobiology gets more and more complicated, its functional expression, which we call the mind, shall get more vivid and productive, extending the frontiers of human understanding all together.

However, without the fundamental and primal capacity of responding to our environment, all of this would cease to exist. In short, regardless of the place of origin, life persists if it can respond and adapt to its environment – and that's where lies the most rudimentary definition as well as the purpose of life – in response and adaptation. And in adaptation lie inclusion and acceptance.

10. WHY DIVERSITY MATTERS

Life on earth is around 3.5 billion years old, and in this aspect, the earth is not much older than that. Our planet formed as a hot mass of molten rock about 4.6 billion years ago. As the earth cooled, much of the water vapor present in its atmosphere condensed into liquid water, which accumulated on the surface in chemically rich oceans.

One scenario for the origin of life is that it originated in this dilute, hot smelly soup of ammonia, formaldehyde, formic acid, cyanide, methane, hydrogen sulfide, and organic hydrocarbons. Whether at the oceans' edge, in hydrothermal deep-sea vents, or elsewhere, the consensus among scientists is that life arose spontaneously from these early waters less than 4 billion years ago. While the way in which this happened still remains a puzzle, one cannot escape a certain curiosity about the earliest steps that eventually led to the origin of all living things on earth, including ourselves.

In this case, all we can do is keep searching and not give in to mystical non-sense, due to our lack of knowledge beyond a certain point. Remember, this threshold of human understanding never remains stagnant, it always keeps moving a step further, turning a little of the unknown into known, bit by bit.

In an attempt to speculate how life might have originated, so far, we scientists have concocted two possible hypotheses. One hypothesis suggests that life may not have originated on earth at all, instead, it may have reached earth from some other planet. This hypothesis is known as the theory of panspermia. Another hypothesis, known as the theory of spontaneous origin, suggests that life evolved spontaneously from inanimate matter, as associations among molecules became more and more complex.

The theory of panspermia proposes that meteors or cosmic dust may have carried significant amounts of complex organic molecules to earth, kicking off the evolution of life. Hundreds of thousands of meteorites and comets are known to have slammed into the early earth, and recent findings suggest that at least some may have carried organic materials.

Most of us scientists tentatively accept the theory of spontaneous origin, that life evolved from inanimate matter. In this view, as changes in molecules increased their stability and caused them to persist longer, these molecules could initiate more and more complex associations, culminating in the evolution of cells around 3.5 billion years ago. These cells got more and more complex over time and eventually gave rise to the wide array of living creatures on earth, including us humans.

Now try to comprehend the gravitas of the matter - one (or a few) tiny little cell lavished an entire planet with millions of various lifeforms. Why? Because it wanted to live – because it wanted to leave a mark of itself – because it couldn't contain its drive for living within itself – it had to bring that drive out and make life sprout in a grand scale. Now fast forward to about 3 billion years, and you have a planet which is so rich with life that we haven't even yet succeeded in identifying and classifying all the species living with us.

Now how did this diversity of life forms take place? It was through the process of genetic mutation – through the mutation of the genes, the building blocks of life, composed of DNA fragments (or, in the case of some viruses, RNA).

Mutation has led to the rich diversity of life that we see all around us, and of which we are a part. And on top of that, diversity is also the reason why our body can fight against pathogens, as mutation is involved in the development of our immune system. It has also provided us food, clothing, and even medicine (through various compounds from plants and through experimentation on animal specimens, which we couldn't possibly conduct on humans).

Diversity has added colors to this world – it has added sweetness to this world – it has added beneficial differences to this world – yet we just can't seem to shake off our un-acceptance of differences. Diversity is the reason why the humankind was able to hoist the flag of equality and justice all around the world higher than ever.

Think about the reign of the idea of nonviolent resistance for example. Tolstoy was a Caucasian, Gandhi was an Asian, and Martin Luther King Jr. was a Negro, yet all of their hearts were inspired by the one idea of nonviolent resistance. King received it from Gandhi, Gandhi received it from Tolstoy, and Tolstoy received it from Christ. And thus behold, we have a world, that's less discriminatory, that's less segregational, that's less prejudicial.

As a species, we have wasted a lot of our time on this planet holding on to the purely discriminatory and non-variant versions of our exclusively personal realities. Great many ages have passed this way – and it made us lose a lot – our sisters, our brothers, our loved ones – all because, while some of us were trying to hold on to our own "pure" "personal" world, others were doing the same. And all through history it has only led to death and destruction. And after all this, if we still can't whole-heartedly embrace the beauty and the magnificence of diversity, then I am sad to say that we don't deserve to call ourselves human.

11. THE ETERNAL DILEMMA

The human species lives in a miasma of internal conflicts – we don't like limitations, yet we crave for limitations, the moment we sense even the possibility of the absence of limitations – because limitlessness means a whole new unknown territory, and anything unknown scares us to death – it's a subconscious reminder of absolute annihilation. Hence, we keep seeking order in disorder – we keep seeking pattern in chaos. The unknown frightens us, so, despite the fact that we boast about ideas like freedom, we are instinctually inclined to dislike them in practice.

As a result, we have imposed more limitations on ourselves than nature imposed on us through selective pressure. We create our own chains with which we bind ourselves and then we keep yelling as raving lunatics, why are we not free? Just once – once, make an effort to demolish the limitations that you have imposed on yourself – and you will see a world which you have never seen before.

The world looks full of joy when we are joyful – the world looks miserable when we are in misery – so, for the world to be able to free itself from miseries that mostly rise from self-imposed limitations, we must first free ourselves from such limitations – not all though, because the mind cannot exist without certain limitations, but there are a whole lot of limitations that we could live without – these are the limitations that rise from absolute obedience or attachment to terms – such as, race, religion, gender, sexuality, empiricism, reductionism, rationalism, fundamentalism, communism, nationalism, capitalism and so on. Unless we break the spell under which we have been living since the time we spread across the world from a corner of Africa, we cannot truly rise as "Sapiens" or "Wise".

Wisdom or enlightenment is not white, black or brown – it's not christian, muslim, jew, hindu or atheist – it's not homosexual or heterosexual – it's not reductionist, empirical or sentimental – it's not belief or disbelief. True enlightenment or wisdom or understanding or insight, whatever we call it, is beyond all opposites – it's beyond materialism and spiritualism – it's beyond atheism and theism – it's beyond all intellectualism and cynicism.

Only when we can see past all arguments - all thesis and anti-thesis, can true productive insight of a phenomenon or a situation manifest in our mind. Mother nature had no blueprint of life, yet it has given rise to this rich and wide kingdom of life. Likewise, we must become wise enough to know the true place for blueprints or maps. The point is, maps have no conscience of their own, just like technology has no conscience of its own, so it all ultimately depends on us, how, where and to what extent we are going to use the maps that we have developed ourselves.

Especially treading on unknown territories, our maps may turn useless, at that time, we will have to depend on the organic apparatus called our mind. And in this endeavor, it's more important to be able to accept failures and errors than to be too sure of oneself. From failure to failure, from error to error, we must explore the infinity of truth – not as proud and intelligent intellectuals, but as naive, curious and childish creatures of conscience.

12. PERILS OF GENIUS

Despite being loved by millions of my sisters and brothers around the world, there are still those who cannot accept me as a scientist, because I have no formal training. The following statement reflects one such notion that I have come across most recently.

"He is a "neuroscientist" in his twenties with no formal training, who has published some thirty books in which he claims to have unlocked the scientific key to individual fulfilment and global harmony. In other words, a crackpot."

Here I am not bothered the slightest bit by the criticism itself, as I receive many of them on a daily basis, alongside letters of appreciation and admiration. But what does bother me here is the disgusting narrow-mindedness that it reflects. According to these childish notions, knowledge and insight can only come from conventional sources.

But the problem here is that, if that were true, we wouldn't have any science to take pride in, in the first place, because many of the achievements that laid the very foundation of science were made by underdogs - by upstarts. Had Hardy denied the genius of Ramanujan, because he had no formal training, then the world of Mathematics would have never received one of its most extraordinary champions.

Just imagine the heaps of letters from thousands of Ramanujans that must be gathering dust on the desks of various university professors. I myself had sent countless letters to many academics during my making with a little hope for support, but with no result, because I was a nobody.

The point is, it's easy to admire a genius after he is recognized, but what's hard is to recognize a genius in the making. Imagine how many Ramanujans and Naskars must have given up hope, because no one gave them a hand that they desperately needed!

In this context, I can remember another person - Satyendranath Bose. Although he was not an autodidact, his work wouldn't have gained the exposure and stature that it did, had Einstein not recognized his potential and brought the name Bose in the sight of the scientific community by placing it next to his. Einstein's collaboration with Bose not only made Bose a household name in the scientific world, but it also revealed to us the greatness of Einstein as a human being.

However, many people often like to proclaim most intellectually that if a person has potential then he or she would be recognized sooner or later. This is nothing but a fallacy, a fairytale that is used to cover up people's inability to help a budding genius. When people are incapable of something, their brain comes up all sorts of fairytale "philosophies" to cover up that incapability.

The world of knowledge and insight is more congested today than ever. So many works are being published today that no one researcher can read all of them. So, in such circumstances, having potential means nothing, because unless your potential is recognized by a popular figure with a stature of his own, chances are that that potential will perish in anonymity.

So, despite knowing this, if you still desire to make an impact on the world, then the only path available to you is to keep working, independent of the expectation of reward or recognition from the world. You might just get lucky and your work might come to the notice of a few individuals, and from them a few more, and from those few the whole world. It's a gamble, but it's a gamble worth taking.

Outside the observation of the mind, there is no such thing as destiny, there is no such thing as order, but only fortunate accidents born out of an infinity of chaos. We are the ones who can turn chaos into pattern - disorder into order - potential into progress. Every step of ours holds the power to influence the world we live in. And by influencing the world I don't mean creating some online profile and posting some trending pictures and photographs in an effort to build a monetizable "influencer" image. A person can have a million followers on instagram by posting fake beauty or fashion content, but this only coaxes a bunch of possession-obsessed humans to buy more things than they need, it doesn't have any impact whatsoever on human progress in the long run – in short, the thing you call today influencing in the world of social media, is actually no influencing.

So, let's investigate a little the process of "influence" in its actual tangible sense. There is no one assured way to influence the world - you can influence the world with literature - you can influence the world with art - you can influence the world with inventing or innovating useful technology - you can influence the world with responsible journalism – you can influence the world with filmmaking - you can influence the world by being a voice of reason, equality and justice - basically you can influence the world in countless ways - no one way is superior to another - each has its distinct possibilities and potential. It all ultimately depends on your own sense of responsibility towards the world. To bring up a passage from my book **The Constitution of The United Peoples of Earth:**

"The whole civilized world runs on trust - people trust journalists to provide accurate information, doctors to provide accurate treatment, scientists to provide accurate answers and solutions to unanswered questions and unsolved problems, pilots to provide safe and fast air transportation, and so on. So, the integrity of the civilized world is predicated on the integrity of the individual in their chosen field of work. Upon their sense of responsibility depends the healthy functioning of an entire species."

13. Beyond Paradigms

A paradigm change will not solve the problems of the human society, but only postpone them, because every paradigm, every system, has its own limitations. So, what we really need is a complete makeover of our very psychological dependencies on paradigms - we must break free from the very urge to rely completely on any certain paradigm. We can use certain elements of a paradigm as we see fit, but we must never become slaves to our paradigms. In fact, all the bloodshed and atrocities committed by the humans, were caused by their loyalty to their own paradigms, to their own systems.

True enlightenment lies in the liberation from all paradigms, psychologically that is. We can still keep on using paradigms, but we must never give any paradigm the exclusive authority of life on earth. And any so-called intellectual who sees this to be a falsifiable hypothesis, I pity them, because despite spending countless hours in the contemplation of various phenomena of this world, they seem to have very little understanding of the necessities of life.

To hell with paradigm, life comes first. There is a term called "starstruck", that is, when you come face to face with a celebrity whom you've admired for a long time, you often freeze and can't utter a word. Likewise, the intellectuals (not all) are paradigm-struck - their paradigm is their prison. To them their paradigm comes first, then human life. Now here I am not attempting to create mistrust towards the intellectuals, rather I am pointing out, what ultimately matters and what not. Let me elaborate this with a little thought experiment.

Imagine a king is lost in the desert. He keeps roaming the desert all day and finally kneels down out of exhaustion and thirst. Suddenly he notices that a man passing, dressed in shabby clothes and carrying a water bottle on his shoulder. The king runs towards the poor man in excitement and begs him for some water, saying "please, give me some water, I'm dying of thirst". The poor man says, "what will you give me in return?" The king says "I'll give you hundred bucks when I get back to my kingdom." "Is that all your life is worth - a hundred bucks", replies the poor man. The king says "okay, I'll give you a thousand bucks." The poor man still doesn't agree. Then out of desperation the king bows before the poor man and says out loud, "I'll give you my entire kingdom, please save my life, I don't have anything else to give". The poor man then gently grabs hold of the king's shoulders and gives him the water, saying, "see, you have nothing significant with which you can buy the water I have, because nothing is worth more than a life, not a hundred bucks, not thousand bucks, not a billion bucks."

In the desert, one who has water is the king, likewise, in 21st century, one who has an active conscience and mettle in character is the true enlightened being - the true kindred spirit - the true human.

And the qualities that make humans human, are beyond the computability of some digital machines - they are neither quantifiable nor falsifiable, yet without them all our technological, mathematical and scientific achievements turn meaningless. Simulation applies to machines, not life. Quantification applies to matter, not sentiments. Falsification applies to theories of science, not to values of life. In fact, it's the values of life, that should guide the theories of science, not the other way around.

Virtues, values, sentiments, reasoning - all of these collectively compose the faculty we call free will. And whether free will is an illusion or not, depends on what you mean by illusion. Does illusion mean the absence of something, if so, then are the sentiments and values that you hold most dear are illusion as well! The point is, here the very term "illusion" is irrelevant. To put it simply, free will is no more illusion than your sentiments are. But, since all our psychological elements are the product of the beautiful and awe-inspiring organ called the brain, malfunction of various brain regions can cause malfunction in those elements. Hence, the capacity of free will depends on the healthy functioning of the brain.

As I first proposed in my book **What is Mind?:**

"The question – do we have free will, itself is not appropriate. We should mend our perspective a little, and start asking the question, do we have the freedom of will, based on our experience?"

Who we are depends on what we learn and remember. Every day you gather information about the world, and that information transforms you into a more learned version of yourself, than the previous day. If certain choice in life makes you suffer immensely with not much expected positive outcome, you get conditioned to avoid making the same choice again in the future. Thus, a choice that you made freely due to lack of experience and futuristic vision, is not going to be repeated once you learn about the downsides of that choice. Hence, given the same situation again in the future, the more experienced version of you will make a different choice, probably a better one, based on all your past experiences.

So, the conclusion is that in every walk of life, you do have the freedom to choose, but that freedom is based on the perception of the world and of yourself, which you have gained until that moment of life. Nature gives you the freedom to choose. But that choice always leads to one ultimate goal - becoming a better version of yourself. Freedom of will is born from the neurons. And that freedom allows you to sometimes make even the worst decisions in life. And by making the worst decision, you simply learn what would be the better decision in future.

So, the capacity of free will, is not some fixed capacity that never changes, rather it keeps evolving based on the experiences you gather over time. Freedom of will is flexible, freedom of will is mendable - based on the information that the brain gathers over time and based on the internal state of the brain. If your brain is stable and healthy, then you'd make better willful decisions, compared to the times when your brain is unstable and unhealthy. Unhealthy mental elements such as grief or anger can substantially alter your willful decisions. Hence, it is not about whether you have free will, rather it is about whether you have enough experience and a stable enough mind to make the best possible willful decision in the current moment of life.

Natural Sciences are all about fascinating causality. But it is not merely causation, it is much more than that. Causality is the amazing foundation, on which all phenomena of life and everything else take shape. And the purpose of natural sciences is to understand the mechanisms underneath causality with intricate detail.

We the scientists take pleasure in attempting to understand things that have baffled humanity since its birth. And the freedom of will in our neurobiology enables us to keep looking, never ever to stop, despite the fact that the search of truth and understanding is an infinite adventure. The continuity of our cellular processes allows our mind to evolve and be better with each passing moment - thus it reveals to us little by little only trace amounts of the reflection of truth.

We are a fantastic species run by biology. Biology is run by intricate cellular mechanisms. Cellular mechanisms are run by Nature. Thus, the more we attempt to understand Nature, the more we get closer to our existential properties. Nature holds the record of our past. And it also holds the key to our future.

And in our pursuit of advancement, we must never lose that original touch with nature. Nature doesn't belong to us, we belong to nature. Understanding nature, gives us insight - understanding nature, gives us wisdom - understanding nature, gives us humility. And with that power of humility and wisdom flowing through our veins, we will one day reach even the Alpha Centaury.

Advancement is good, advancement is necessary, but in the pursuit of advancement, we must never forget why we are making the advancement in the first place! We must always keep asking the question, what sort of advancement do we want - a cold, mechanical and elitist advancement for only a handful of rich, resourceful and egotistical snobs or a warm, wise and healthy advancement for all of humankind!

With all the powers bestowed in us by Mother Nature, I have no doubt that one after another, we will one day unravel most of the secrets of the universe both external and internal, but upon reaching the fountain-head of knowledge and advancement, when we look back at the days of struggle, it's our footsteps that should appear in our memories, not our lost humanity. Forget not, humanity without humanity, is no humanity, no matter how advanced it is. More than machines, we need mindfulness - more than likes, we need kindness - more than connections, we need commitment - more than advancement, we need enlightenment.

BIBLIOGRAPHY

Archer M., (2000), Being Human: The Problem of Agency. Cambridge University Press.

Archer M., (2003), Structure, Agency and the Internal Conversation. Cambridge University Press.

Adolphs R (2003) Cognitive neuroscience of human social behaviour. Nature Rev Neurosci 4: 165–178.

Adolphs R, Tranel D, Damasio AR (2003) Dissociable neural systems for recognizing emotions. Brain Cogn 52: 61–69.

Afton, A. D. (1985). Forced copulation as a reproductive strategy of male lesser scaup: A field test of some predictions. - Behaviour 92, p. 146-167.

Allison T, Puce A, McCarthy G. (2000) Social perception from visual cues: role of the STS region. Trends Cogn Sci 4: 267–278.

Andresen, Jensine, and Robert Forman, eds. Cognitive Models and Spiritual Maps. Bowling Green, Ohio: Imprint Academic, 2000.

Ashbrook, James, and Carol Albright. The Humanizing Brain: Where Religion and Neuroscience Meet. Cleveland, OH: Pilgrim Press, 1997.

Azari, Nina, Janpeter Nickel, Gilbert Wunderlich, Michael Niedeggen, Harald Hefter, Lutz Tellmann, Hans Herzog, Petra Stoerig, Dieter Birnbacher, and Rudiger Seitz. "Neural Correlates of Religious Experience." European Journal of Neuroscience 13, no. 8 (2001)

Agar, N. (2004). Liberal eugenics: In defence of human enhancement. London: Blackwell Publishing.

Alteheld, N., Roessler, G., Vobig, M., & Walter, R. (2004). The retina implant new approach to a visual prosthesis. Biomedizinische Technik, 49(4), 99–103.

Antal, A., Nitsche, M. A., Kincses, T. Z., Kruse, W., Hoffmann, K. P., & Paulus, W. (2004a). Facilitation of visuo-motor learning by transcranial direct current stimulation of the motor and extrastriate visual areas in humans. European Journal of Neuroscience, 19(10), 2888–2892.

Bhat Z, Kumar, S, Bhat H (2015) In vitro meat production. Challenges and benefits over conventional meat production. J Sci Food Agric 14: 241–248

Bernstein R. J., (1967), John Dewey. New York: Washington Square Press.

Bernstein R.J., (1971), Praxis and Action: Contemporary Philosophies of Human Activity. Philadelphia: University of Pennsylvania Press.

Bernstein R.J., (1976), The Restructuring Social and Political Thought.

Bernstein R.J., (1983), Beyond Relativism and Objectivism: Science, Hermeneutics, and Praxis. Philadelphia: University of Pennsylvania Press.

Bernstein R.J., (1986), Philosophical Profiles. Philadelphia: University of Pennsylvania Press.

Bernstein R.J., (1991), New Constellation. Cambridge: MIT Press.

Barash, D. P. (1977). Sociobiology of rape in mallards (Anas platyrhynchos): Responses of the mated male. - Science 197, p. 788-789.

Berger, J. (1986). Wild horses of the great basin: Social competition and population size. - The University of Chicago Press, Chicago.

Birkhead, T. R., Johnson, S. D. & Nettleship, D. N. (1985). Extra-pair matings and mate guarding in the common murre Uria aalge. - Anim. Behav. 33, p. 608-619.

Beauregard, Mario, and Vincent Paquette. "Neural Correlates of a Mystical Experience in Carmelite Nuns." Neuroscience Letters 405, no. 3 (2006)

Benson, Herbert. Timeless Healing: The Power and Biology of Belief. New York: Scribner, 1996

Bogen, J.E.(1995a), 'On the neurophysiology of consciousness: Part I. An overview', Consciousness and Cognition, 4.

Bogen, J.E. (1995b), 'On the neurophysiology of consciousness: Part II. Constraining the semantic problem', Consciousness and Cognition, 4.

Bremner, J. D., R. Soufer, et al. (2001). "Gender differences in cognitive and neural correlates of remembrance of emotional words." Psychopharmacol Bull 35 (3).

Brothers, L. (2002). The social brain: A project for integrating primate behavior and neurophysiology in a new domain. In J. T. Cacioppo et al. (Eds.), Foundations in neuroscience. Cambridge, MA: MIT Press.

Buss, D. D. (2003). Evolutionary Psychology: The New Science of Mind, 2nd ed. New York: Allyn & Bacon.

Buss, D. M. (1989). "Conflict between the sexes: Strategic interference and the evocation of anger and upset." J Pers Soc Psychol 56 (5).

Buss, D. M. (1995). "Psychological sex differences. Origins through sexual selection." Am Psychol 50 (3).

Buss, D. M. (2002). "Review: Human Mate Guarding." Neuro Endocrinol Lett 23 (Suppl 4).

Buss, D. M., and D. P. Schmitt (1993). "Sexual strategies theory: An evolutionary perspective on human mating." Psychol Rev 100 (2).

Blakemore SJ, Decety J (2001) From the perception of action to the understanding of intention. Nature Rev Neurosci 2: 561.

Bruce C, Desimone R, Gross CG (1981) Visual properties of neurons in a polysensory area in superior temporal sulcus of the macaque. J Neurophysiol 46: 369–384.

Buccino G, Vogt S, Ritzl A, Fink GR, Zilles K, Freund HJ, Rizzolatti G (2004) Neural circuits underlying imitation of hand actions: an event related fMRI study. Neuron 42: 323–34.

Colapietro V., (1988), "Human Agency: The Habits of Our Being."

Southern Journal of Philosophy, XXVI, 2, pp. 153-68.

Colapietro V., (1992), "Purpose, Power, and Agency." The Monist, 75, 4 (October) pp. 423-44.

Colapietro V., (2003), "Signs and their vicissitudes: Meanings in excess of consciousness and functionality." Logica, Dialogica, Ideologica, a cure di Susan Petrilli e Patrizia Calefato (Milano: Mimesis), pp. 221-36.

Colapietro V., (2004a), "C. S. Peirce's Reclamation of Teleology." Nature in American Philosophy, ed. Jean De Groot (Washington, D.C.: Catholic University Press of America), pp. 88-108.

Colapietro V., (2004b), "Portrait of a Historicist: An Alternative Reading of Peircean Semiotic." Semiotiche, 2/04 [maggio 2004], pp. 49-68.

Colapietro V., (2006), "Engaged Pluralism: Between Alterity and

Sociality." The Pragmatic Century: Conversations with Richard J. Bernstein (Albany, NY: SUNY Press), pp. 39-68.

Colapietro V., (2009), "Habit, Competence, and Purpose." Forthcoming in The Transactions of the Charles S. Peirce Society. Calder AJ, Keane J, Manes F, Antoun N, Young AW (2000) Impaired recognition and experience of disgust following brain injury. Nature Neurosci 3: 1077–1078.

Carey DP, Perrett DI, Oram MW (1997) Recognizing, understanding and reproducing actions. In: Jeannerod M, Grafman J (eds) Handbook of neuropsychology. Vol. 11: Action and cognition. Elsevier, Amsterdam.

Carr L, Iacoboni M, Dubeau MC, Mazziotta JC, Lenzi GL (2003) Neural mechanisms of empathy in humans: a relay from neural systems for imitation to limbic areas. Proc Natl Acad Sci USA 100: 5497–5502.

Changeux JP, Ricoeur P (1998) La nature et la règle. Odile Jacob, Paris.

Cochin S, Barthelemy C, Roux S, Martineau J (1999) Observation and execution of movement: similarities demonstrated by quantified electroencephalograpy. Eur J Neurosci 11: 1839– 1842.

Chomsky Noam, (2017) Requiem for the American Dream

Chomsky Noam, (2016) Who Rules the World?

Chomsky Noam, (2010) How the World Works

Churchland, P.S. (1986), Neurophilosophy (Cambridge, MA: The MIT Press).

Churchland, P.S. & Ramachandran, V.S. (1993), 'Filling in: Why Dennett is wrong', in Dennett and His Critics:

Demystifying Mind, ed. B. Dahlbom (Oxford: Blackwell Scientific Press).

Churchland, P.S., Ramachandran, V.S. & Sejnowski, T.J. (1994), 'A critique of pure vision', in Large- scale Neuronal Theories of the Brain, ed. C. Koch & J.L. Davis (Cambridge, MA: The MIT Press).

Crick, F. (1994), The Astonishing Hypothesis: The Scientific Search for the Soul (New York: Simon and Schuster).

Crick, F. (1996), 'Visual perception: rivalry and consciousness', Nature, 379.

Crick, F. & Koch, C. (1992), 'The problem of consciousness', Scientific American, 267.

Craig AD (2002) How do you feel? Interoception: the sense of the physiological condition of the body. Nature Rev Neurosci 3: 655–666.

Damasio, A (2003a) Looking for Spinoza. Harcourt Inc. Damasio A (2003b) Feeling of emotion and the self. Ann NY Acad Sci 1001: 253–261.

d'Aquili, Eugene. "Senses of Reality in Science and Religion." Zygon 17, no 4 (1982)

d'Aquili, Eugene. "The Biopsychological Determinants of Religious Ritual Behavior." Zygon 10, no. 1 (1975)

d'Aquili, Eugene. "The Myth-Ritual Complex: A Biogenetic Structural Analysis." Zygon 18, no. 3 (1983)

d'Aquili, Eugene, and Andrew Newberg. The Mystical Mind: Probing the Biology of Religious Experience. Minneapolis: Fortress Press, 1999.

Daly DD. 1958. Ictal affect. Am J Psychiatry.

Damasio, A. (1994) Descartes' Error: Emotion, Reason and the Human Brain. New York, Putnams.

Damasio, A. (1999) The Feeling of What Happens: Body, Emotion and the Making of Consciousness. London, Heinemann.

Darwin, C. (1859) On the Origin of Species by Means of Natural Selection. London, Murray.

Darwin, C. (1871) The Descent of Man and Selection in Relation to Sex. London, John Murray.

Darwin, C. (1872) The Expression of the Emotions in Man and Animals. London, John Murray; also published 1965, Chicago, University of Chicago Press.

Dawkins, M.S. (1987) Minding and mattering. In C. Blakemore and S. Greenfield (eds) Mindwaves. Oxford, Blackwell, 151-60.

Dawkins, R. (1976) The Selfish Gene. Oxford, Oxford University Press; a new edition, with additional material, was published in 1989.

Dawkins, R. (1986) The Blind Watchmaker. London, Longman.

Di Pellegrino G, Fadiga L, Fogassi L, Gallese V, Rizzolatti G (1992) Understanding motor events: A neurophysiological study. Exp Brain Res 91: 176–80.

Deikman, A.J. (2000) A functional approach to mysticism. Journal of Consciousness Studies 7(11-12), 75-91.

Delmonte, M.M. (1987) Personality and meditation. In M. West (ed.) The Psychology of Meditation. Oxford, Clarendon Press, 118-32.

Dennett, D.C. (1987) The Intentional Stance. Cambridge, MA, MIT Press.

Dennett, D.C. (1988) Quining qualia. In A.J. Marcel and E. Bisiach (eds)

Consciousness in Contemporary Science. Oxford, Oxford University Press, 42-77.

Dennett, D.C. (1991) Consciousness Explained. Boston, MA, and London, Little, Brown and Co.

Dennett, D.C. (1995a) Darwin's Dangerous Idea. London, Penguin.

Dennett, D.C. (1995b) The unimagined preposterousness of zombies. Journal of Consciousness Studies 2(4), 322-6.

Dennett, D.C. (1995c) Cog: steps towards consciousness in robots. In T. Metzinger (ed.) Conscious Experience. Thorverton, Devon, Imprint Academic, 471-87.

Dennett, D.C. (1995d) The path not taken. Behavioral and Brain Sciences 18, 252-3; commentary on N. Block, On a confusion about a function of consciousness. Behavioral and Brain Sciences 18, 227.

Dennett, D.C. (1996a) Facing backwards on the problem of consciousness. Journal of Consciousness Studies 3(1), 4-6.

Dennett, D.C. (1996b) Kinds of Minds: Towards an Understanding of Consciousness. London, Weidenfeld & Nicolson.

Dennett, D.C. (1997) An exchange with Daniel Dennett. In J. Searle (ed.) The Mystery of Consciousness. New York, New York Review of Books, 115-19.

Dennett, D.C. (1998) The myth of double transduction. In S.R. Hameroff, A.W. Kaszniak and A. C. Scott (eds) Toward a Science of Consciousness: The Second Tucson Discussions and Debates. Cambridge, MA, MIT Press, 97-107.

Dennett, D.C. (1998b) Brainchildren: Essays on Designing Minds. Cambridge, MA, MIT Press.

Dennett, D.C. (2001) The fantasy of first person science. Debate with D. Chalmers, Northwestern University, Evanston, IL, February 2001.

Dennett, D.C. (2003) Freedom Evolves. New York, Penguin.

Dennett, D.C. and Kinsbourne, M. (1992) Time and the observer: the where and when of consciousness in the brain. Behavioral and Brain Sciences 15, 183-247, including commentaries and authors' responses.

Dewey J., (1911 [1977]), "Epistemological Realism: The Alleged Ubiquity of the Knowledge Relation." Journal of Philosophy, VIII, 20 (September 28, 1911).

Dewhurst, Kenneth, and A. W. Beard. "Sudden Religious Conversions in Temporal Lobe Epilepsy." British Journal of Psychiatry 117 (1970)

Dewhurst K, Beard AW. Sudden religious conversions in temporal lobe epilepsy. 1970 Epilepsy Behav 2003

Devinsky O, Lai G. Spirituality and religion in epilepsy. Epilepsy Behav 2008.

Devinsky, O., Morrell, MJ, Vogt, BA. (1995) 'Contribution of anterior cingulate cortex to behavior', Brain, 118.

Douglas Stone A., Chapter 24, The Indian Comet, in the book Einstein and the Quantum, Princeton University Press, Princeton, New Jersey, 2013.

E. Horvitz, "One Hundred Year Study on Artificial Intelligence: Reflections and Framing," ed: Stanford University, 2014.

Einstein A. (1925). "Quantentheorie des einatomigen idealen Gases". Sitzungsberichte der Preussischen Akademie der Wissenschaften.

Eckhart Meister, Selected Writings

Egidi R., ed. (1999), "Von Wright and 'Dante's Dream': Stages in a Philosophical Pilgrim's Progress", in In Search of a New Humanism: the Philosophy of G.H. von Wright, ed. by R. Egidi, Kluwer, Dordrecht.

Fadiga L, Fogassi L, Pavesi G, Rizzolatti G (1995) Motor facilitation during action observation: a magnetic stimulation study. J Neurophysiol 73: 2608–2611.

Fogassi L, Gallese V, Fadiga L, Rizzolatti G (1998) Neurons responding to the sight of goal directed hand/arm actions in the parietal area PF (7b) of the macaque monkey. Soc Neurosci Abs 24:257.5.

Frith U, Frith CD (2003) Development and neurophysiology of mentalizing. Philos Trans R Soc Lond B Biol Sci 358: 459.

Farah, M.J. (1989), 'The neural basis of mental imagery', Trends in Neurosciences, 10.

Finlay BL, Darlington RB (1995) Linked regularities in the development and evolution of mammalian brains. Science 268.

Freud, S. "The Interpretation of Dreams", 1900

Freud, S. "Selected papers on hysteria and other psychoneuroses" Journal of Nervous and Mental Disease 1909.

Freud, S. "The Origin and Development of Psychoanalysis", 1910

Freud, S. "Psychopathology of everyday life", 1914

Freud, S. "Beyond the Pleasure Principle", 1920

Frith, C.D. & Dolan, R.J. (1997), 'Abnormal beliefs: Delusions and memory', Paper presented at the May,

1997, Harvard Conference on Memory and Belief.

Gay, Volney, ed. Neuroscience and Religion. Plymouth, UK: Lexington Books, 2009.

Gazzaniga, M. S. (1985). The social brain. New York: Basic Books.

Gazzaniga, M.S. (1993), 'Brain mechanisms and conscious experience', Ciba Foundation Symposium, 174.

Geschwind N. "Behavioural changes in temporal lobe epilepsy". Psychol Med. 1979.

Gellhorn, E., Kiely, W.F. "Mystical states of consciousness: neurophysiological and clinical aspects." J Nerv Ment Dis. 1972;154:399-405.

Gilbert SL, Dobyns WB, Lahn BT (2005) Genetic links between brain development and brain evolution. Nat Rev Genet 6.

Gray JA. The Psychology of Fear and Stress. 2nd ed. New York, NY: Cambridge University Press; 1988.

Gloor, P. (1992), 'Amygdala and temporal lobe epilepsy', in The Amygdala: Neurobiological Aspects of Emotion, Memory and Mental Dysfunction, ed J.P. Aggleton (New York: Wiley-Liss).

Greenspan, S. I. and S. G. Shanker (2004). The first idea: How symbols, language, and intelligence evolved from our early primate ancestors to modern humans. Cambridge, MA: Da Capo Press.

Grady, D. (1993), 'The vision thing: Mainly in the brain', Discover, June.

Gallagher HL, Frith CD (2003) Functional imaging of 'theory of mind'. Trends Cogn Sci 7: 77.

Gallese V, Fogassi L, Fadiga L, Rizzolatti G (2002) Action representation and the inferior parietal lobule. In: Prinz W, Hommel B (eds) Attention & Performance XIX. Common mechanisms in perception and action. Oxford University Press, Oxford.

Gallese V, Keysers C, Rizzolatti G (2004) A unifying view of the basis of social cognition. Trends Cogn Sci 8: 396–403.

Gangitano M, Mottaghy FM, Pascual-Leone A (2001) Phase specific modulation of cortical motor output during movement observation. NeuroReport 12: 1489–1492.

Gangitano M, Mottaghy FM, Pascual-Leone A (2004) Modulation of premotor mirror neuron activity during observation of unpredictable grasping movements. Eur J Neurosci 20: 2193– 2202.

Goldman AI, Sripada CS (2004) Simulationist models of face-based emotion recognition. Cognition 94: 193–213.

Grèzes J, Costes N, Decety J (1998) Top-down effect of strategy on the perception of human biological motion: a PET investigation. Cogn Neuropsychol 15: 553–582.

Grèzes J, Armony JL, Rowe J, Passingham RE (2003) Activations related to "mirror" and "canonical" neurones in the human brain: an fMRI study. Neuroimage 18: 928–937.

Gross CG, Rocha-Miranda CE, Bender DB (1972) Visual properties of neurons in the inferotemporal cortex of the macaque. J Neurophysiol 35: 96–111.

Hari R, Forss N, Avikainen S, Kirveskari S, Salenius S, Rizzolatti G (1998) Activation of human primary motor cortex during action observation: a neuromagnetic study.

Proc. Natl Acad Sci USA 95: 15061–15065.

Hardy, G. H. (1940). Ramanujan. Cambridge: Cambridge University Press.

Hall, Daniel, Keith Meador, and Harold Koenig. "Measuring Religiousness in Health Research: Review and Critique." Journal of Religion and Health 47, no. 2 (2008)

Harris, Sam, Jonas Kaplan, Ashley Curiel, Susan Bookheimer, Marco Iacoboni, and Mark Cohen. "The Neural Correlates of Religious and Nonreligious Belief." PLoS One 4, no. 10 (October 1, 2009)

Halgren, E. (1992), 'Emotional neurophysiology of the amygdala within the context of human cognition', in The Amygdala: Neurobiological Aspects of Emotion, Memory and Mental Dysfunction, ed J.P. Aggleton (New York: Wiley-Liss).

Halligan PW, Fink GR, Marshal JC, Vallar G. 2003. Spatial cognition: evidence from visual neglect. Trends Cogn Sci.

Handbook of Emotions, Edited by Michael Lewis, Jeannette M. Haviland-Jones, and Lisa Feldman Barrett, The Guilford Press; 3rd edition (2010).

Haggard, P., Clark, S. and Kalogeras,]. (2002) Voluntary action and conscious awareness, Nature Neuroscience 5, 382-5. Haggard, P., Newman, C. and Magno, E. (1999) On the perceived time of voluntary actions. British Journal of Psychology 90, 291-303.

Hameroff, S.R. and Penrose, R. (1996) Conscious events as orchestrated space-time selections. Journal of Consciousness Studies 3(1), 36-53; also reprinted in J. Shear (ed.) (1997) Explaining Consciousness-The Hard Problem. Cambridge, MA, MIT Press, 177-95.

Hardcastle, V.G. (2000) How to understand theN in NCC. InT. Metzinger (ed.) Neural Correlates of Consciousness. Cambridge, MA, MIT Press, 259-64.

Harding, D.E. (1961) On Having no Head: Zen and the Re-Discovery of the Obvious. London, Buddhist Society.

Hardy, A. (1979) The Spiritual Nature of Man: A Study of Contemporary Religious Experience. Oxford, Clarendon Press.

Hamad, S. (1990) The symbol grounding problem. Physica D 42, 335-46.

Hamad, S. (2001) No easy way out. The Sciences 41(2), 36-42.

Harre, R. and Gillett, G. (1994) The Discursive Mind. Thousand Oaks, CA, Sage.

Haugeland, J. (ed.) (1997) Mind Design II: Philosophy, Psychology, Artificial

Intelligence. Cambridge, MA, MIT Press.

Hauser, M.D. (2000) Wild Minds: What Animals Really Think. New York, Henry Holt and Co.; London, Penguin.

Hearne, K. (1990) The Dream Machine. Northants, Aquarian.

Hebb, D.O. (1949) The Organization of Behavior. New York, Wiley.

Helmholtz, H.L.F. von (1856-67) Treatise on Physiological Optics.

Hess, EH (1975) "The role of pupil size in communication," Scientific American, 233(5), 110–12.

Heyes, C.M. (1998) Theory of mind in nonhuman primates. Behavioral and Brain Sciences 21, 101-48; with commentaries.

Heyes, C.M. and Galef, B.G. (eds) (1996) Social Learning in Animals: The Roots of Culture. San Diego, CA, Academic Press.

Hilgard, E.R. (1986) Divided Consciousness: Multiple Controls in Human Thought and Action. New York, Wiley.

Hocquette JF (2016) Is in vitro meat the

solution for the future? Meat Science 120:

167–176

Hodgson, R. (1891) A case of double consciousness. Proceedings of the Society for Psychical Research 7, 221-58.

Hofstadter, D.R. (1979) Code!, Escher, Bach: An Eternal Golden Braid. London, Penguin.

Hofstadter, D.R. and Dennett, D.C. (eds) (1981) The Mind's I: Fantasies and Reflections on Self and Soul. London, Penguin.

Holland, J. (ed.) (2001) Ecstasy: The Complete Guide: A Comprehensive Look at the Risks and Benefits of

MDMA. Rochester, VT, Park Street Press.

Holmes, D.S. (1987) The influence of meditation versus rest on physiological arousal. In M. West (ed.) The Psychology of Meditation. Oxford, Clarendon Press, 81-103.

Holt, J. (1999) Blindsight in debates about qualia. Journal of Consciousness Studies 6(5), 54-71.

Horgan, J. (1994), 'Can science explain consciousness?', Scientific American, 271.

Holloway RL (1996) Evolution of the human brain. In: Lock A, Peters CR (eds) Handbook of human symbolic evolution. Oxford University Press, Oxford

Iacoboni M, Woods RP, Brass M, Bekkering H, Mazziotta JC, Rizzolatti G (1999) Cortical mechanisms of human imitation. Science 286: 2526–2528.

Iacoboni M, Koski LM, Brass M, Bekkering H, Woods RP, Dubeau MC, Mazziotta JC, Rizzolatti G (2001) Reafferent copies of imitated actions in the right superior temporal cortex. Proc Natl Acad Sci USA 98: 13995–13999.

Jeannerod M (1988) The neural and behavioural organization of goal-directed movements. Clarendon Press, Oxford.

Johnson-Frey SH, Maloof FR, Newman-Norlund R, Farrer C, Inati S, Grafton ST (2003) Actions or hand-objects interactions? Human inferior frontal cortex and action observation. Neuron 39: 1053–1058.

Jackson, F. (1982) Epiphenomenal qualia. Philosophical Quarterly 32, 127-36.

James, W. (1890) The Principles of Psychology (2 volumes). London, Macmillan.

James, W. (1902) The Varieties of Religious Experience: A Study in Human Nature. New York and London, Longmans, Green and Co.

Jansen, K. (2001) Ketamine: Dreams and Realities. Sarasota, FL, Multidisciplinary Association for Psychedelic Studies.

Jay, M. (ed.) (1999) Artificial Paradises: A Drugs Reader. London, Penguin.

Jaynes, J. (1976) The Origin of Consciousness in the Breakdown of the Bicameral Mind. New York, Houghton Mifflin.

Johnson, M.K. and Raye, C.L. (1981) Reality monitoring. Psychological Review 88, 67-85.

Kadim I, Mahgoub O, Baqir S et al. (2015) Cultured meat from muscle stem cells: a review of challenges and prospects. J Integr Agr 14: 222–233

Koski L, Iacoboni M, Dubeau MC, Woods RP, Mazziotta JC (2003) Modulation of cortical activity during different imitative behaviors. J Neurophysiol 89: 460–471.

Krolak-Salmon P, Henaff MA, Isnard J, Tallon-Baudry C, Guenot M, Vighetto A, Bertrand O, Mauguiere F (2003) An attention modulated response to disgust in human ventral anterior insula. Ann Neurol 53: 446–453.

Kandel, E. R. In Search of Memory: The Emergence of a New Science of Mind, W. W. Norton & Company (2007).

Kandel E. R. Schwartz JH, Jessel TM. Principles of neural sciences. New York; McGraw Hill, 2000.

Kanizsa, G. (1979), Organization In Vision (New York: Praeger).

Kaloupek DG, Scott JR, Khatami V. Assessment of coping strategies associated with syncope in blood donors. J Psychosom Res. 1985;29:207-214.

Kanwisher, N. (2001) Neural events and perceptual awareness. Cognition 79, 89-113; also reprinted inS. Dehaene (ed.) The Cognitive Neuroscience of Consciousness. Cambridge, MA, MIT Press, 89-113.

Kapleau, Roshi P. (1980) The Three Pillars of Zen: Teaching, Practice, and Enlightenment (revised edn). New York, Doubleday.

Karn, K. and Hayhoe, M. (2000) Memory representations guide targeting eye movements in a natural task. Visual Cognition 7, 673-703.

Kasamatsu, A. and Hirai, T. (1966) An electroencephalographic study on the Zen meditation (zazen). Folia Psychiatrica et Neurologica Japonica 20, 315-36.

Kaiserman-Abramof, I. R., Graybiel, A. M., & Nauta, W. J. (1980). The thalamic projection to cortical area 17 in a congenitally anophthalmic mouse strain. Neuroscience, 5, 41–52.

Kanold, P. O., Kara, P., Reid, R. C., & Shatz, C. J. (2003). Role of subplate neurons in functional maturation of visual cortical columns. Science, 301, 521–525.

Kennedy, H., & Dehay, C. (1988). Functional implications of the anatomical organization of the callosal projections of visual areas V1 and V2 in the macaque monkey. Behav. Brain Res., 29, 225–236.

Kentridge, R.W. and Heywood, C.A. (1999) The status of blindsight. Journal of Consciousness Studies 6(5), 3-11.

Kihlstrom, J.F. (1996) Perception without awareness of what is perceived, learning without awareness of what is learned. In M. Velmans (ed.) The Science of Consciousness. London, Routledge, 23-46.

Kollerstrom, N. (1999) The path of Halley's comet, and Newton's late apprehension of the law of gravity. Annals of Science 56, 331-56.

Kosslyn, S.M. (1980) Image and Mind. Cambridge, MA, Harvard University Press.

Kosslyn, S.M. (1988) Aspects of a cognitive neuroscience of mental imagery. Science 240, 1621-6.

Kinsbourne, M. (1995), 'The intralaminar thalamic nucleii', Consciousness and Cognition, 4.

Kjaer, Troels, Camilla Bertelsen, Paola Piccini, David Brooks, Jorgen Alving, and Hans Lou. "Increased Dopamine Tone during Meditation- Induced Change of Consciousness." Cognitive Brain Research 13, no. 2 (April 2002)

Kölmel HW. 1985. Complex visual hallucinations in the hemianopic field. J Neurol Neurosurg Psychiatry.

Koenig, Harold. "Research on Religion, Spirituality, and Mental Health: A Review." Canadian Journal of Psychiatry 54, no. 5 (May 2009)

Koenig, Harold, ed. Handbook of Religion and Mental Health. San Diego, CA: Academic Press, 1998

Kraepelin E. Psychiatry: A Textbook for Students and Physicians. New York, NY: Science History Publications; 1990.

Lauglin, Charles, John McManus, and Eugene d'Aquili. Brain, Symbol, and Experience. 2nd ed. New York: Columbia University Press, 1992

Lakoff, G. and M. Johnson (1999). Philosophy in the flesh. Basic Books: New York.

LeDoux, J. E. (1996). The emotional brain. New York: Simon & Schuster.

LeDoux, J.E. (1992), 'Emotion and the amygdala', in The Amygdala:

Neurobiological Aspects of Emo- tion, Memory and Mental Dysfunction, ed J.P. Aggleton (New York: Wiley-Liss).

Levin, D.T. and Simons, D.J. (1997) Failure to detect changes to attended objects in motion pictures. Psychonomic Bulletin and Review 4, 501-6.

Levine,J. (1983) Materialism and qualia: the explanatory gap. Pacific Philosophical Quarterly 64, 354-61.

Levine,J. (2001) Purple Haze: The Puzzle of Consciousness. New York, Oxford University Press. Levine, S. (1979) A Gradual Awakening. New York, Doubleday.

Levinson, B.W. (1965) States of awareness during general anaesthesia. British Journal of Anaesthesia 37, 544-6.

Lewicki, P., Czyzewska, M. and Hoffman, H. (1987) Unconscious acquisition of complex procedural knowledge. Journal of Experimental Psychology: Learning, Memory and Cognition 13, 523-30.

Lewicki, P., Hill, T. and Bizot, E. (1988) Acquisition of procedural knowledge about a pattern of stimuli that cannot be articulated. Cognitive Psychology 20, 24-37.

Lewicki, P., Hill, T. and Czyzewska, M. (1992) Nonconscious acquisition of information. American Psychologist 47, 796-801.

Manthey S, Schubotz RI, von Cramon DY (2003). Premotor cortex in observing erroneous action: an fMRI study. Brain Res Cogn Brain Res 15: 296–307.

Mesulam MM, Mufson EJ (1982) Insula of the old world monkey. III: Efferent cortical output and comments on function. J Comp Neurol 212: 38–52.

Naskar, Abhijit. "Homo: A Brief History of Consciousness", 2015

Naskar, Abhijit. "What is Mind?", 2016

Naskar, Abhijit. "In Search of Divinity: Journey to The Kingdom of Conscience", 2016

Naskar, Abhijit. "Love, God & Neurons: Memoir of A Scientist who found himself by getting lost", 2016

Naskar, Abhijit. "Neurons of Jesus: Mind of A Teacher, Spouse & Thinker", 2017

Naskar, Abhijit. "The Islamophobic Civilization: Voyage of Acceptance", 2017

Naskar, Abhijit. "Principia Humanitas", 2017

Naskar, Abhijit. "We Are All Black: A Treatise on Racism", 2017

Naskar, Abhijit. "Wise Mating: A Treatise on Monogamy", 2017

Naskar, Abhijit. "Illusion of Religion: A Treatise on Religious Fundamentalism", 2017

Naskar, Abhijit. "I Am The Thread: My Mission", 2017

Naskar, Abhijit. "Morality Absolute", 2017

Naskar, Abhijit. "Fabric of Humanity", 2018

Naskar, Abhijit. "The Constitution of The United Peoples of Earth", 2019

Naskar, Abhijit. "Neurons Giveth, Neurons Taketh Away | Abhijit Naskar | TEDxIIMRanchi", 2019 https://www.youtube.com/watch?v=B NX-Q0ySm80

Newberg, Andrew, and Jeremy Iversen. "The Neural Basis of the Complex Mental Task of Meditation: Neurotransmitter and Neurochemical Considerations." Medical Hypotheses 61, no. 2 (2003).

Newberg, Andrew. "How God Changes Your Brain: An Introduction to Jewish Neurotheology", CCAR Journal: The Reform Jewish Quarterly, Winter 2016.

Newberg, Andrew, and Stephanie Newberg. "A Neuropsychological Perspective on Spiritual Development." In Handbook of Spiritual Development in Childhood and Adolescence, edited by Eugene Roehlkepartain, Pamela King, Linda Wagener, and Peter Benson. London: Sage Publications, Inc., 2005

Newberg, Andrew. "The Neurotheology Link An Intersection Between Spirituality and Health", Alternative and Complimentary Therapies, Vol 21 No 1, February 2015.

Newberg, Andrew, Nancy Wintering, Dharma Khalsa, Hannah Roggenkamp, and Mark Waldman. "Meditation Effects on Cognitive Function and Cerebral Blood Flow in

Subjects with Memory Loss: A Preliminary Study." Journal of Alzheimer's Disease 20, no. 2 (2010)

Nash, M. (1995), 'Glimpses of the mind', Time.

Nesse RM. Proximate and evolutionary studies of anxiety, stress and depression: synergy at the interface. Neurosci Biobehav Rev. 1999;23:895-903.

Nicolelis, Miguel. (2011) "Beyond Boundaries: The New Neuroscience of Connecting Brains with Machines---and How It Will Change Our Lives", Times Books

O'Hara, K. and Scutt, T. (1996) There is no hard problem of consciousness. Journal of Consciousness Studies 3(4), 290-302, reprinted in J. Shear (ed.) (1997) Explaining Consciousness. Cambridge, MA, MIT Press, 69-82.

O'Regan, J.K. (1992) Solving the "real" mysteries of visual perception: the world as an outside memory. Canadian Journal of Psychology 46, 461-88.

O'Regan, J.K. and Noe, A. (2001) A sensorimotor account of vision and visual consciousness. Behavioral and Brain Sciences 24(5), 883-917.

O'Regan, J.K., Rensink, R.A. and Clark,].]. (1999) Change-blindness as a result of "mudsplashes." Nature 398, 34.

Ornstein, R.E. (1977) The Psychology of Consciousness (2nd edn). New York, Harcourt.

Ornstein, R.E. (1986) The Psychology of Consciousness (3rd edn). New York, Pehguin.

Ornstein, R.E. (1992) The Evolution of Consciousness. New York, Touchstone.

Penfield W, Faulk ME (1955) The insula: further observations on its function. Brain 78: 445– 470.

Penrose, R. (1994), Shadows of the Mind (Oxford: Oxford University Press).

Penrose, R. (1989), The Emperor's New Mind: Concerning Computers, Minds and The Laws of Physics (Oxford: Oxford University Press).

Persinger, "'I would kill in God's name' role of sex, weekly church attendance, report of a religious experience and limbic lability" Perceptual and Motor Skills 1997.

Persinger "Experimental simulation of the God experience" Neurotheology 2003.

Persinger, M. A. (1993b). Personality changes following brain injury as a grief response to the loss of sense of self: Phenomenological themes as indices of local lability and neurocognitive restructuring as psycho- therapy. Psychological Reports, 72

Persinger, Corradini, Clement, Keaney, et al "Neurotheology and its convergence with neuroquantology" NeuroQuantology 2010.

Persinger, Koren and St-Pierre "The electromagnetic induction of mystical and altered states within the laboratory" Journal of Consciousness Exploration and Research 2010.

Persinger "Case report: A prototypical spontaneous 'sensed presence' of a sentient being and concomitant electroencephalographic activity in the clinical laboratory" Neurocase 2008.

Persinger and Saroka "Potential production of Hughlings Jackson's "parasitic consciousness" by physiologically-patterned weak transcerebral magnetic fields: QEEG and source localization" Epilepsy & Behavior 28 (2013).

Persinger. "The neuropsychiatry of paranormal experiences". J Neuropsychiatry Clin Neurosci 2001.

Persinger. "Neuropsychological bases of god beliefs", New York: Praeger, 1987

Persinger. "Temporal lobe epileptic signs and correlative behaviors displayed by normal populations", Journal of General Psychology, 1986

Perry BD, Pollard R. Homeostasis, stress, trauma, and adaptation. A neurodevelopmental view of childhood trauma. Child Adolesc Psychiatr Clin N Am. 1998;7:33.

Paré, D. & Llinás, R. (1995), 'Conscious and preconscious processes as seen from the standpoint of sleep-waking cycle neurophysiology', Neuropsychologia, 33.

P. S. de Laplace. Essai Philosophique sur les Probabilites [1814], in Academy des Sciences, Oeuvres Complotes de Laplace, Vol. 7, Gauthier-Villars, Paris (1886).

Perrett DI, Harries MH, Bevan R, Thomas S, Benson PJ, Mistlin AJ, Chitty AJ, Hietanen JK, Ortega JE (1989) Frameworks of analysis for the neural representation of animate objects and actions. J Exp Bio 146: 87–113.

Phillips ML, Young AW, Senior C, Brammer M, Andrew C, Calder AJ, Bullmore ET, Perrett DI, Rowland D, Williams SC, Gray JA, David AS (1997) A specific neural substrate for perceiving facial expressions of disgust. Nature 389: 495–498.

Phillips ML, Young AW, Scott SK, Calder AJ, Andrew C, Giampietro V, Williams SC, Bullmore ET, Brammer M, Gray JA (1998) Neural responses to facial and vocal expressions of fear and disgust. Proc R Soc Lond B Biol Sci 265: 1809–1817.

Puce A, Perrett D (2003) Electrophysiological and brain imaging of biological motion. Philosoph Trans Royal Soc Lond, Series B, 358: 435–445.

Ramachandran VS. Behavioral and magnetoencephalographic correlates of plasticity in the adult human brain. Proc Natl Acad Sci USA 1993; 90: 10413–20.

Ramachandran VS. Phantom limbs, neglect syndromes, repressed memories, and Freudian psychology. Int Rev Neurobiol 1994; 37: 291–333.

Ramachandran VS. Plasticity and functional recovery in neurology. Clin Med 2005; 5: 368–73.

Ramachandran VS, Hirstein W. The perception of phantom limbs. The D. O. Hebb lecture. Brain 1998; 121: 1603–30.

Ramachandran VS, Rogers-Ramachandran D, Cobb S. Touching the phantom limb. Nature 1995; 377: 489–90.

Ramachandran VS, Rogers-Ramachandran D. Phantom limbs and neural plasticity. Arch Neurol 2000; 57: 317–20.

Ramachandran VS, Rogers-Ramachandran D. It's all done with mirrors. Sci Am Mind 2007; 18: 16–9.

Ramachandran VS, Rogers-Ramachandran D. Sensations referred to a patient's phantom arm from another subjects intact arm: perceptual correlates of mirror neurons. Med Hypotheses 2008; 70: 1233–4.

Ramachandran VS, Rogers-Ramachandran D, Stewart M. Perceptual correlates of massive cortical reorganization. Science 1992; 258: 1159–60.

Rizzolatti G, Craighero L (2004) The mirror-neuron system. Annu Rev Neurosci 27: 169–192.

Rizzolatti G, Fogassi L, Gallese V (2001) Neurophysiological mechanisms underlying the understanding and imitation of action. Nature Rev Neurosci 2:661–670.

Rock I, Victor J. Vision and touch: an experimentally created conflict between the two senses. Science 1964; 143: 594–6.

Rose´n B, Lundborg G. Training with a mirror in rehabilitation of the hand. Scand J Plast Reconstr Surg Hand Surg 2005; 39: 104–8.

Royet JP, Plailly J, Delon-Martin C, Kareken DA, Segebarth C (2003) fMRI of emotional responses to odors: influence of hedonic valence and judgment, handedness, and gender. Neuroimage 20: 713–728.

Rozin R Haidt J and McCauley CR (2000) Disgust. In: Lewis M, Haviland-Jones JM (eds) Handbook of Emotion. 2nd Edition. Guilford Press, New York, pp 637–653.

Saxe R, Carey S, Kanwisher N (2004) Understanding other minds: linking developmental psychology and functional neuroimaging. Annu Rev Psychol 55: 87–124.

S. J. Russell and P. Norvig, Artificial intelligence: a modern approach (3rd edition): Prentice Hall, 2009.

Schienle A, Stark R, Walter B, Blecker C, Ott U, Kirsch P, Sammer G, Vaitl D (2002) The insula is not specifically involved in disgust processing: an fMRI study. Neuroreport 13: 2023–2026.

Showers MJC, Lauer EW (1961) Somatovisceral motor patterns in the insula. J Comp Neurol 117: 107–115.

Singer T, Seymour B, O'Doherty J, Kaube H, Dolan RJ, Frith CD (2004) Empathy for pain involves the affective but not the sensory components of pain. Science 303: 1157–1162.

Smith A (1759) The theory of moral sentiments (ed. 1976). Clarendon Press, Oxford.

S. N. Bose (1924). "Plancks Gesetz und Lichtquantenhypothese". Zeitschrift für Physik. 26 (1): 178–181.

Sprengelmeyer R, Rausch M, Eysel UT, Przuntek H (1998) Neural structures associated with recognition of facial expressions of basic emotions Proc R Soc Lond B Biol Sci 265: 1927–1931.

Strafella AP, Paus T (2000) Modulation of cortical excitability during action observation: a transcranial magnetic stimulation study. NeuroReport 11: 2289–2292.

Simonsen R (2015) Eating for the future: veganism and the challenge of in vitro meat. In: Stapleton P, Byers A (Hg). Biopolitics and utopia. Palgrave Macmillan, New York (2015), S 167–190

Tanaka K (1996) Inferotemporal cortex and object vision. Ann Rev Neurosci. 19: 109–140.

Tesla N. "My Inventions", 1919

T. R. Society, "Machine learning: the power and promise of computers that learn by example," ed. The Royal Society, 2017.

Tomasello M, Call J (1997) Primate cognition. Oxford University Press, Oxford.

Tremblay C, Robert M, Pascual-Leone A, Lepore F, Nguyen DK, Carmant L, Bouthillier A, Theoret H (2004) Action observation and execution: intracranial recordings in a human subject. Neurology. 63: 937–938.

Umilta MA, Kohler E, Gallese V, Fogassi L, Fadiga L, Keysers C, Rizzolatti G (2001) "I know what you are doing": a neurophysiological study. Neuron 32: 91–101.

Von Wright G.H., (1963), Norm and Action. A Logical Inquiry, Routledge & Kegan Paul, London.

Von Wright G.H., (1976), "Determinism and the Study of Man", in Essays on Explanation and Understanding, ed. by J. Manninen and R. Tuomela, Reidel, Dordrecht.

Von Wright G.H., (1977), "What is Humanism?", The Lindlay Lecture, University of Arkansas, Lawrence, Kansas.

Von Wright G.H., (1979), "Humanism and the Humanities", in Philosophy and Grammar, ed. by S. Kanger and S. Öhman, Reidel, Dordrecht, pp. 1-16. Reprinted in von Wright (1993).

Von Wright G.H., (1980), Freedom and Determination, North-Holland Publishing Co., Amsterdam.

Von Wright G.H., (1985), Of Human Freedom, The Tanner Lectures on Human Values,

Vol. VI, ed. by S. M. McMurrin, University of Utah Press, Salt Lake City, pp. 107-70. Reprinted in von Wright (1998).

Von Wright G.H., (1993), The Tree of Knowledge and Other Essays, Brill, Leiden.

Von Wright G.H., (1997), "Progress: Fact and Fiction", in The Idea of Progress, ed. by A. Burgen et al., W. de Gruyter, Berlin, pp. 1-18.

Von Wright G.H., (1998), In the Shadow of Descartes: Essays in the Philosophy of Mind, Kluwer, Dordrecht.